WEALTH CREATION

THE MINDSET

The mindset is the doorway to the heart of your wealth creation.

Rob Wilson

(Wealth Creation - The Mindset)
Copyright © 2022 by (Wealth Accumulation Concepts)

ISBN 978-0-9721065-3-5

Printed in the USA

Dedication

These series of Wealth Creation is dedicated to the many families that I have comes across in my work. It is also dedicated to you the now reader, whether you are reading just this book or the entire series, I am in prayer that you experience wealth creation personally.

I especially wish that you who have chosen to read this series find what they are seeking.

To:

_____

Rob Wilson

W

H

Y

?

Sometimes it is your why that matters. Sometimes you have to know why. Sometimes you learn this/that is why.

Know your WHY.

Table of Contents

Foreword

'By wisdom a house is built, and through understanding it is established; through knowledge its rooms are filled with rare and beautiful treasures.' -Proverbs 24:3-4

I have known Rob since some of my earliest conscious memories. My foggy vision of these past memories see Rob in our old church's basement in an apron serving with the kitchen volunteers. He would come over and serve my family's table and put up with me and sometimes a friend's teasing, giving as good as he was getting!

Over 20 years and two church buildings later, most of my encounters with Rob are while he is doing what he's always done—serve—oftentimes while he's wearing an apron. Over the course of over 20 years, maybe 1000 encounters, and countless conversations, I have noticed two consistent things about Rob: 1) He delights in serving people 2) He is a lover of knowledge and wisdom, especially as it pertains to wealth.

This project is coming from who Rob is and has always been as long as I can remember. You will read the work of a man who has a heart to serve people and has sought out wealth wisdom and knowledge over the course of decades. Here, he is serving the food of knowledge and wisdom to nourish your mind and ultimately, your life. In this work, Rob shares wisdom to change

i

how you think about money because he knows that to live well means to deal with money wisely. It is not his love of money, but his love for people and how they live that has driven him to create this work. He has seen the mental, emotional, and relational turmoil that can arise from unwise perspectives, presumptions, and practices surrounding money and this book is an answer that leads to flourishing instead of suffering, abundance instead of scarcity.

'If the foundations be destroyed what can the righteous do?' - Psalm 11:3 Rob understands the importance of starting from a strong and true foundation, which is why the first installment of this series is about your foundation—your mindset. We cannot live beyond our level of thinking. How we think is also how we see.

How we see determines what we do. In this work, Rob diagnoses common destructive ideas and perspectives in our mental foundation that give rise to distorted visions and destructive patterns that cause financial ruin.

More than merely diagnosing diseased financial concepts, he provides us with curing principles that give rise to healthy financial thinking and seeing. This book will help you to lay a foundation for your financial life by leading you to wise ways of thinking about money. If we can think better, we can see better.

If we can see better, we can do better. If you apply the knowledge and wisdom found in this book, it can change not only your financial life, but your whole life.

-Dale Carnegie Bronner II

Preface

Are you looking to learn more about wealth creation in your life? It all starts with your money mindset! I am writing this series to help you change your money mindset—but not from scarcity to abundance because that hasn't worked for you in the past. It really will not be difficult for you to create wealth when you know the right strategy.

So, how will you change your money mindset to make powerful money decisions?

I will share five foundational principles in this series to help you change your mindset about wealth creation, not just abundance. These are principles that will change your money mindset.

Our mind is very powerful, and when used the right way, we can turn our life around. Keep reading to learn how to transform your money mindset to wealth creation.

Introduction

In my book, "Wealth Increasing Now," I desperately tried to lay the foundation that wealth is created and not the result of a gift from a rich uncle or lottery winnings. It is a fact that a huge number of millionaires earned their millions by working for it. The work begins with the mindset more than the amount of money they earn.

I really hope that you get this next statement:

The mindset is a collection of preconceived notions that a person has built based on influences affecting them, like family, personal experience, media, education, and the unknown. In other words, it is the set of beliefs a person has that establishes his or her mindset.

Mindsets can be used to put people in groups. I talk about the wealth mindset or poverty mindset in "Wealth Increasing Now." Wealth or poverty mindset all relates to the popular "Law of Attraction" theory.

The theory of a wealth mindset is spending less, making wise investments, and looking for ways to improve financial standing with minimal risk affecting your personal financial reality.

The theory of poverty mindset is the belief that there isn't enough of anything to go around: not enough money, time, planning, leaders, clean air, rest, love—not enough of just about anything that a person wants, that they think they need, or anything that is important to them.

The mindset creates a vision of "WHY," "WHO," "WHAT," "WHERE," and "WHEN." Wealth Creation is a process of many different traits, habits, and characteristics blended together to produce a desired result.

The vision of wealth creation is more than thinking about money and how much you can get. Let me be clear about something here: Wealth can mean many different things to people. Money is simply the currency needed to make an exchange for goods or services, while wealth is the abundance of money or material possessions. Wealth is the sum total of assets (things that you own) that gives you financial security. The word wealth **SHOULD** carry the idea of abundance and security.

Wealth, abundance, and security often seem to flow more easily for some people without much effort. They have the practices and principles that lead them into a mindset of prosperity. When one taps into the potential that surrounds them, they are able to develop a prosperity mindset.

This Wealth Creation series was written to provide you with the practices and principles that can shift you into a mindset of prosperity. The wealth creation mindset involves how people feel about money. It depends on how they will take action and what they will focus on each day. It involves having the ability to shift away from a desire for more prosperity and into a mindset in which one's thoughts easily support wealth and abundance.

I want you to start releasing contradictory feelings and the nature of sabotaging behaviors preventing you from being receptive to something greater and focus on results intended to help you be more effective in reaching your financial goals. It is critical to move from feelings of lack to feelings of abundance in order to develop financial prosperity and wealth creation with greater ease.

Wealth Creation is something to be experienced every day. When people have an open and receptive mindset to new ways of being and doing that creates value, more wealth flows into their life.

Chapter One - The Mental

Money is mental!

I know people who have struggled all of their life with finances. Most of the time, they were buried in debt, and the rest of the time, they had just enough to survive. Looking back over many clients, they all would say, "I could blame my parents. They always had just enough because their mindset was: Having enough is enough for us."

This is amusing to me. They never ever blamed themselves for accepting such a narrow mindset.

There are many people out there who would be very happy with having just enough money, especially the ones who struggle to pay their bills every month. Having a limited belief about money or wealth creation can hold you back a lot in life.

Think about it this way, having enough money will get you the absolute minimum. It will be enough to pay the bills, but you will not have enough funds to save money. It will put food on the table, but you will not be able to try new things, eat out in fancy restaurants, or take care of your health (buying high-quality organic food).

The mindset is always impacted in some way. Many people get caught in the cycle of working hard for their money but not having enough money (or time) to educate themselves and learn new things. They work hard and are able to take annual vacations, on which they drive six hours by car to stay in a 3-star hotel, but are still unable to explore the world, visit new places, travel in business class, or arrive well-rested in a beautiful hotel or 5-star resort.

You see, having enough money may be enough to survive, but it is not enough to live life to the fullest. Until your money mindset changes, you will NOT fully experience life, leading to unhappiness and constantly searching for something else. Your mindset must be changed.

Most people believe that having the right money mindset is something you are born with, but that's not true. A healthy money mindset is something you can learn through training, just as almost everything in life. Once you master this skill, manifesting money will be easy.

People with a poverty mindset generally take one of two positions with money. One is that they have no respect for money at all. Why would anyone disrespect or not appreciate money? In this Wealth Creation series, I will attempt to address these positions or issues.

If you want money to save you, you should save it. Most people will go about their lives daily without giving saving money a single thought.

Most people run out of money at the end of every month or are constantly scraping to get by. They have no idea what amount they should spend on food, entertainment, clothing, etc.

Very often, they do not know how much money is coming in each month, and they can't for the life of them tell you where their money is going. It's just not that important to them.

Their rob-Peter-to-pay-Paul mentality puts them squarely in a hole that consistently creates hardship as opposed to being set aside for retirement and an emergency fund. (Notice, I did not say Wealth Creation.)

If you ignore money and disrespect your finances, you will be playing a game of Russian Roulette, resulting in financial hardships that cannot be reversed. When money is not respected, there is likely no clear vision in the spender's mind.

I know of families that simply have no respect for their own money but will seek money from others to help them when their financial lives are falling apart. Each month, the light or gas bills are scheduled for disconnection, but they somehow find a way to broadcast their new tattoo or body piercing.

Money is really mental. There are reports that mental health and money problems are often intricately linked. Research has shown that millions of people are experiencing both of these issues: debt and mental health.

People with debt problems are significantly more likely to experience mental health problems. This is a scary thought, but there really is a link.

The Mental

Does being in financial difficulty affect your mental health? You bet it does. Financial difficulties are a common cause of stress and anxiety. The stigma around debt can mean that people struggle to ask for help and may become isolated.

Isolation creates a deep conversation about money. Studies have offered conflicting evidence. One study suggests that people with higher incomes spend less time socializing and another suggests they feel less lonely.

But what about the working-class people? I believe lower-income people are more likely to experience isolation and a lower sense of belonging than higher-income people.

Overall, people with higher incomes spend less time socializing and more time alone. At the same time, their time spent socializing is more often with friends than with family.

Poverty has shaped the perceptions of people with lower incomes. Their personal experiences of stigmatization and isolation leads to mental health issues.

The impact on people's mental health can be particularly severe if they resort to cutting back on essentials, such as heating and eating, or if their creditors are aggressive or insensitive when collecting debts.

Financial difficulty drastically reduces recovery rates for common mental health conditions. People with depression and bad debt are 4.2 times more likely to still have depression 18 months later than people without financial difficulty.

People with debt problems are three times as likely to have thoughts about suicide. The recent pandemic has caused more people to commit suicide. There is rarely one single factor that drives people to take their own life.

There is typically a range of social issues, life events, and cognitive and personality factors combined. However, there is a strong link between debt problems and suicide.

Sadly, during the recent pandemic, grants and other free money initiatives supported self-isolation. There were even food subsidies and housing allowances for people to stay home. The impact has not been measured yet.

Do mental health problems affect your income? The income gap for those with mental health problems is significant. People with anxiety and depression have a median gross annual income of $8,400 less than people without those conditions.

When it comes to working, people with mental health problems are more likely to work part-time and are overrepresented in low-paying roles. It is overlooked in the mental health space. People with mental health problems are in the three lowest paid occupational groups.

People with mental health problems are more likely to receive financial benefits that provide support. This support could be housing benefits or out-of-work benefits for common mental disorders such as depression or anxiety disorder.

The Mental

Severe episodes of mental health issues can also disrupt incomes. People can struggle to attend work, maintain their benefit claims, or stay on top of managing their money.

People can struggle with mounting debt from medical bills for their mental health care, including amassing thousands in debt for the care provided by their crisis team.

I know it is hard to consider mental health as an issue related to money. However, mental health problems affect expenditure and the ability to save. Even memory issues can make it harder to stay on top of financial management.

Many people's spending patterns and ability to make financial decisions change significantly during poor mental health periods. This change increases the likelihood of financial difficulty and makes financial decisions harder.

The simple struggle of memory loss can cause one to put off paying bills or take out a loan that they would not have otherwise taken out. As a financial coach, it took me many years before I realized this as a fact.

There will be many references to the mental side of the mindset. Most people function with some form of mental health issue while others struggle severely.

People can struggle to understand bills and remember account details, leading to financial difficulties and distress.

Some functional individuals can only make ends meet for less than a month if their household loses its main source of income.

Mental health problems can affect your ability to access essential services and manage your finances. They can also make it harder to engage with essential services like banks and energy companies.

As I write this series, I am thinking of a support system that can play a vital role in tackling financial difficulties for people with mental health problems. I pray this book serves as a lifeline to people with debt problems, but some people with mental health problems will still struggle to access debt advice and get the critical help they need.

Do you shop online when you feel lonely? Are you constantly worried about money?

Most people would say they work hard to earn money. However, your emotional relationship with cash determines how hard your money works for you. Everyone has a personal psychological relationship with money that influences decisions about how to spend it, save it, or invest it.

Are you making the right choices?

Since our personal finances are usually a very private part of our lives, it can be hard to recognize potentially damaging patterns of behavior.

For example, are you always the person who offers to pay at the end of a meal with friends? Or, do you earn a fortune in finance yet never spend money on new clothes? Perhaps you are an investor. Could your frequent trading tip over into a gambling addiction? Or, could you be spending beyond your means to boost your self-esteem?

Taking the Financial Times' money psychology quiz could provide the insight you need. Rate how strongly you agree or disagree, with the following statements, from -3 (strongly disagree) to +3 (strongly agree).

Your answers will reveal which of the six common types of financial personalities you most closely match up to and what to do about it. Visit https://ig.ft.com/sites/quiz/psychology-of-money/ for your results.

1. I get a real kick out of the business of managing my money.

-3	0	+3
Strongly disagree	Neutral/not sure	Strongly agree

2. I follow the trends in money management.

-3	0	+3
Strongly disagree	Neutral/not sure	Strongly agree

3. I am very generous with the people I love.

-3	0	+3
Strongly disagree	Neutral/not sure	Strongly agree

4. Having a lot of money is a sign of success.

-3	0	+3
Strongly disagree	Neutral/not sure	Strongly agree

5. I feel safe and secure if I have a lot of money saved.

-3	0	+3
Strongly disagree	Neutral/not sure	Strongly agree

6.   I'm puzzled a lot over money decisions.

-3	0	+3
Strongly disagree	Neutral/not sure	Strongly agree

7. I think I check on my financial affairs more than other people.

-3	0	+3
Strongly disagree	Neutral/not sure	Strongly agree

8. I am constantly re-evaluating my investments.

-3	0	+3
Strongly disagree	Neutral/not sure	Strongly agree

9. I spend money on myself "because I am worth it."

-3	0	+3
Strongly disagree	Neutral/not sure	Strongly agree

10. I admit that I buy things to impress others.

-3	0	+3
Strongly disagree	Neutral/not sure	Strongly agree

11. I prefer to be safe rather than a gambler when it comes to money.

-3	0	+3
Strongly disagree	Neutral/not sure	Strongly agree

12. I am really not interested in money matters.

-3	0	+3
Strongly disagree	Neutral/not sure	Strongly agree

13. There are lots of money bargains, be prepared to search for them.

-3	0	+3
Strongly disagree	Neutral/not sure	Strongly agree

14. I believe investing time in money programs is worthwhile.

-3	0	+3
Strongly disagree	Neutral/not sure	Strongly agree

15. I buy new outfits for special occasions so that I will be dressed appropriately.

-3	0	+3

The Mental

16. You get respect from others when you have lots of money.

-3	0	+3
Strongly disagree	Neutral/not sure	Strongly agree

17. I value having a lot of easy-to-access money in the bank.

-3	0	+3
Strongly disagree	Neutral/not sure	Strongly agree

18. I prefer to let others I trust make important money decisions for me.

-3	0	+3
Strongly disagree	Neutral/not sure	Strongly agree

Chapter Two

Maxing Out Your Income

Here is a story about Lauren. She has always been financially focused. However, after the unexpected death of her husband, her financial life transformed. What were once urges to save became urges to spend. She became torn between keeping the faith in savings and its relation to a good future and enjoying her money here and now.

She now spends her hard-earned money on things she feels will give her instant gratification or happiness while not being mindful of the consequences. She stopped caring enough about the future, feeling she deserved what she blew her money on, only to discover she had made one of the worst money decisions of her life.

She went from living with a monthly surplus of $1,200 to living paycheck to paycheck with an occasional payday loan worked in each month. It doesn't matter what she spent this money on at this point. What matters here is her mindset—the lack of respect for money.

I realize there comes a moment in one's life (and this is especially true for those who have been working hard for a long time and have suffered loss) when one just feels the need to throw caution to the wind and "let go."

After all, when the urge to just **spend it** becomes too strong, you may just give in, thinking "I deserve this," "It's my life,"

"This is **WHY** I work hard," "We only live once," and that common view about money and spending, "It's just money and money cannot buy happiness."

Is this rebellion or disrespect? What would cause a person to stop planning or abandon the idea of a financial future? The drastic big spending decisions are made because they have misinterpreted views about money and its use and purpose.

It is in fact the mindset, the common views about money that makes the difference between those who see money as a tool to enjoy life and those who see it beyond being an instrument of pleasure.

When an individual pushes their income to the limit, they become completely dependent on that next paycheck. It's that feeling of absolute dread that if they were to lose that paycheck there is no grocery or gas money. It's being one emergency away from going deeper into debt. It is stressful and creates a constant baseline of anxiety and insecurity.

I read somewhere recently that more than 40 percent of Americans spend more than they make. I am not at all surprised this has led to a debt-centered financial life. Spending more than what you make **"sells your income"** to the future. It is completely maxing out your income or putting a mortgage on income not yet earned.

Without a plan to catch up to the cost of the money you've already spent, your debt will accumulate more debt through interest. Living month-to-month also creates a situation where you have nothing to fall back on if your money runs out.

Unfortunately, this over-spending lifestyle (mindset) perpetuates the myth that we'll catch up on our debt in the future, keeping people in exactly the same situation year after year.

Spending less than your salary is rarely the model that most people grow up with in the modern world, even though saving up and paying cash keeps us better positioned for the future.

Whether they have a high income or a low income, people are not saving money for the future. Living paycheck to paycheck has become a common way of living and the struggle is not easily seen from the outside.

I can say that almost every household lives the same way. You may not believe it, but even some of the very rich live in the same manner. They all max out their income based on a lifestyle for today, not the future.

Here's the thing: People do not want to plan out their income and expenditure. Organizing and planning for the future seems too complicated. But it is easy to live within any amount of income once you have a clear plan. Unfortunately, it's not a part of the future plan for most.

Monthly income should be dedicated to future planning, present comforts, and saving to reach goals and achieve whatever amount of financial security is desired.

Millennials (OMG) have a drive and tenacity that is off of the charts when thinking about finance and the future. As it turns out, millennials spend their money largely on the same things as anyone else.

To their credit, older millennials have earned less and paid more for necessities like housing and healthcare than their parents, but they have also started saving earlier for financial goals like retirement.

There is a certain confidence in this group. Although they went through the recession and the pandemic, they are somewhat different when it comes to income. Their mindset takes on a whole new look.

I am bringing them into the conversation because I have seen them blow through money as if there were no tomorrow. It could easily seem as though they are living in the fast lane, but that is not true at all.

Some would say their success is followed by a fairly static path: they land a good job, get married, buy a house, and have kids. Millennials have simply started to do things in their own order not that of what their parents may have done.

Their consumption habits are also more likely to be driven by their personal values or morals, like ever-increasing interest in sustainable investing and recent pushes to make workplaces more diverse.

That's partly out of necessity and partly because some want different lives than their parents. For example, they actually consider mental and physical health an essential expense, unlike their parents.

As I write about maxing out your income, it reminds me of a family that I sat down with some years ago. They were facing personal bankruptcy and wanted to find a way to avoid filing chapter 7. We talked about their money situation and the things that were going on in their lives.

Their mentality was totally committed to getting on the right page. They wanted to be in the right position. In order to be able to do the right things, everything had to be positive. The conversation leading up to sitting down to analyze their personal financial situation made me feel good.

The first task was to create a budget to discover the facts: **"WHY"** was this family facing bankruptcy? They lived in a modest home, they had three cars and there were three working adults in the household. So why were they facing personal bankruptcy? What was the reason?

After we sat down and talked about the budget and put everything in place, the next thing I had to do was to free up money in the house so that they were no longer living paycheck to paycheck.

You see, living paycheck to paycheck had become a way of life for them. Many people get in a situation where they have

15

maxed out their income without realizing that it is what they're doing.

This is exactly what I said earlier; it's putting a mortgage on your salary. It puts a liability on your capacity to work and how long you must work in order to meet those obligations.

Back to the family. Once we identified all of the expenditures, I was able to free up some money and then we could see a little daylight. There was a sense of relief, a feeling that they could do this and did not have to file bankruptcy.

Now let's look at the next step of how to eliminate the current liability that they had. The debt that caused the financial hardship in the household was made up of credit card debt, car payments, and payday loans.

Of all the debt they could not afford to pay each month, the biggest one I tackled was the payday loan. We contacted the organization, negotiated a payout settlement, and instead of having to pay $500 in interest every month, they received a reasonable settlement of $1,200 to satisfy the debt.

This one obligation put $500 back into the household. Sadly, adding this $500 back to the household income caused painful havoc and crisis. I watched this family begin to fight over what they would spend this money on—not how to save it, not how to invest it, and not how to take a breather and enjoy not living paycheck to paycheck. It was impossible for them to consider living without financial hardship.

The mindset of all three of the working family members was to spend. Their thinking was to get something new or go on a vacation because they deserved it. They'd been dealing with this hardship for too long.

They did not have any vision or foresight in their lives to say that they wanted to be and do better. I guess the positive talking from our first conversation, including repeatedly saying they wanted to get out of debt, save, and invest, was only to convince me to help.

I was wrong about their commitment to making changes. I did not expect this family to debate about what to do with the $500. Mind you, this $500 wasn't the only money that was freed up in the household.

We identified how to cut back on expenses, including their eating out. They were also able to get their utilities on budget billing and were able to reduce other costs.

After lowering their monthly expenditures, they were looking at a total of about $780 remaining in the household budget and it became a battle every single month to determine what to do with that surplus.

I explained that if they held on to the money for 10 months, they'd have $7,800. If they held on to it for a year, they'd have over $9,000. But they could not envision doing anything close to that. This is why they were maxing out their income.

What do you do if your expenditure exceeds your income? You have to make up the difference by using savings or by borrowing. A person will get into financial trouble if they continue to spend more than their income.

I really hate writing about borrowing money to fix an income related issue. This is how payday loans and personal consumer finance loans create the cycle of financial hardship.

I mentioned a consumer finance loan. So what is it? It is any type of loan where a person borrows money from a lender. There are various types of consumer finance loans that are both secured and unsecured. Each loan comes with different terms and interest rates and they're usually intended for a specific purpose.

These loans are personal loans like fast loans or credit. The defining feature of fast loans, which are not regulated by law, is the speed with which they are granted. Lenders simplify risk analysis procedures which usually translates into higher costs for the customer.

Can borrowing money bail someone out? Yes, it can, but not without a high cost. There must be a change that takes place. It's important for each reader to look deep inside themselves and determine if there are mental or physical actions that need to be considered.

Spending Less Than Your Income

Spending less than your income is good! This is called a surplus. It means you have money left over and are in good shape. When you create your plan with a money map at the beginning of the month, plan to spend less than the expected income. At the end of the month, compare the Total Spending for needs and wants to your actual Total Monthly Income. When there is any remaining money, it can be put toward savings.

Spending More Than Your Income

Spending more than your monthly income is not so good! This is called a deficit. It means you have overspent and it is time to look at where there may be too much spending.

I have created a monthly money map designed to help you clearly see what your income and expenditures are so that you can avoid overspending. If you find yourself spending more than you had for the month, don't panic.

Take a look at where you overspent. Can you cut spending for entertainment? Can you stop eating out? In your money map, commit to spend less on your wants and try to stick to the plan. This is how you control your finances.

Personal Money Map   **Month:** _____

My Needs Descriptions	Planned Spending	Actual Spending
1. _____	$ _____	$_____
2. _____	$ _____	$_____
3. _____	$ _____	$_____
4. _____	$ _____	$_____
5. _____	$ _____	$_____
6. _____	$ _____	$_____
7. _____	$ _____	$_____
8. _____	$ _____	$_____
My Total Needs	$ _____	$_____

My Wants Descriptions	Planned Spending	Actual Spending
1. _____	$ _____	$_____
2. _____	$ _____	$_____
3. _____	$ _____	$_____
4. _____	$ _____	$_____
5. _____	$ _____	$_____
6. _____	$ _____	$_____
My Total Wants	$ _____	$ _____
My Expenses (Total Needs + Total Wants)	$_____	$_____
My Total Monthly Income	$_____	$_____
My Cash Flow (Income – Expenses)	$_____	$_____

Chapter Three

Carrying Too Much Debt

In 2021, most households had debt totaling $92,727 on average, according to consumer reports. This debt figure includes credit card balances, student loans, mortgages, and other types of consumer finance personal loans.

Even without a mortgage, the debt total is still an exceptionally high $57,836. Let's face it, who can afford to put down $250,000 in cash on a new home or $48,000 on a new car? Yet, creating debt is seen as a necessity or as something that appears under control.

Better yet, just rent to own or utilize any other type of rental service where there is no debt being carried. Keep in mind, even if there is no debt incurred when you rent to own, it is a waste of resources. In fact, a person is most likely paying off the asset of another.

However, if it's all kept under control and there is a plan in place to pay everything off, a person is good to go. Problems arise when people accumulate a lot of debt from many different sources and then choose to not have a plan.

It should be scary to acknowledge a lot of debt, and even scarier to figure out how to pay it off. But with the mindset of carrying too much debt, a person simply does not care. This mindset helps one ignore debt and smile. Ignoring debt is asking for poverty and the various hardships that come along with it.

You need to have a plan for how to deal with it before that happens.

Carrying too much debt can begin in many different ways. For example, a college student away from home for the first time could find themselves listening to friends and ignoring their parents' instructions, accepting more financial aid than needed and ending up with student loan debt.

Next, that same college student could begin suffering from self-confidence issues. The struggle is real and they are not comfortable with their appearance, feeling like they don't fit in. To compensate for these feelings, they spend the leftover financial aid funds when it could have been returned. Like many other people, they go to the local mall to buy clothes when feeling sad or depressed.

They try to make themselves feel better, by spending money on getting their nails done, going to tanning salons, visiting expensive hair salons, visiting sporting events, and purchasing gaming systems—anything but saving–in an attempt to feel like they belong.

The mindset of spending quickly causes a downward spiral. It makes you feel good about yourself for a short time. Before long, you return to spending money on ridiculous things, continually needing to find happiness from what you buy.

When a person begins to struggle to make debt payments or their payments are so high that they can't accomplish much else, they may have too much debt.

Even when people can manage their payments, having too much debt can still lead to other financial problems like not being able to save money, missing bill payments, and having to borrow more money just to stay afloat. There are many signs that let people know that they have more debt than can be handled.

Too many people are hiding from their debt as if that will make it go away. The truth is, when someone purposefully starts to ignore their debt, chances are they have more debt than they can handle and they are simply afraid to face up to it. It's likely that they are also under the pressure of being delinquent and late on payments.

When debt payments are higher than income, it's a sure sign of too much debt. Not having enough money for monthly payments leads to missing payments from time to time, which makes the debt problems worse. Paying late leads to higher interest.

Once debt becomes unaffordable and delinquent, debt collectors will start calling. Yes, a person may be able to avoid debt collector phone calls for a while, but they should never underestimate those creditors and debt collectors. They could decide to sue for what is owed and if they win the lawsuit, they may be able to get court permission to garnish wages or levy bank accounts.

In the previous chapter, I talked about loans and the impact they could have as a tax on the income. Paying bills with loans from family, friends, credit cards, or cash advance places only adds to the debt which is already excessive.

Eventually, there will be no other sources to borrow money from. That's when one has to face the debt accumulated with creditors and loved ones. This is never a good feeling, yet the mindset will justify the steps taken to get to that point.

Debt can cause people to be so worried about bills that they can't sleep at night. They toss and turn fretfully wondering how they are going to pay their bills. That's a sure sign that the debt has gotten out of control. I have talked about how debt-related stress can lead to other medical problems. If your debt habits are beyond your control, that may be a sign that you are addicted to debt.

Consider this, when financial woes spill into the workplace, it's time to do things differently. Losing a job is the last thing needed when you have accumulated too much debt because a loss of income could put you over the financial edge. Dealing with debt problems can eliminate stress and in some cases, literally save lives.

I have to mention this: Needing to buy groceries with a credit card shows an even deeper issue—you don't have enough money to sustain your lifestyle. Maybe the problem is not making enough money to begin with or it could be mishandling the money that is made. Either way, it's necessary to figure out how to survive on the income made or increase the income.

Credit card debt is one of those things most people find easy to ignore. After all, nearly everybody has credit cards and most have some experience with maxing-out one of them at one time or another. This is a classic sign of being financially unstable.

A maxed-out credit card is a pure liability. It represents an ongoing monthly payment and is no longer a source of fresh credit.

The reasons for maxing-out credit cards are almost never good. And since the prospect of paying off the maxed-out cards is so remote, it's just a matter of time before you will max out a second card, and then a third, and so on.

Having maxed-out credit cards can cause you to delay or eliminate an important major purchase. This can be anything from replacing your TV, the roof of your house, or replacing your car. No matter how dysfunctional the item may be, you don't replace it because you don't have the money to pay for it.

In extreme cases, this can also cause you to delay a medical procedure or put off getting braces for one of your children. These are large expenses and you won't be able to pay for them if you don't have the extra cash—even if you are otherwise able to pay your regular monthly bills.

If you've maxed out a credit card, that's not a good sign. When you begin maxing-out credit cards, your credit score is likely to drop.

Carrying Too Much Debt

This is because your credit utilization ratio — the amount of money you owe, divided by your available credit — increases. This ratio represents 30% of your credit score calculation.

The ideal threshold on a credit utilization ratio is 30%. That means, if you have revolving lines of credit totaling $30,000, you can have up to $9,000 outstanding without hurting your credit score. As you move beyond the 30% threshold, your credit score will decline, even if you make all your payments on time.

Naturally, a lower credit score will make it more difficult to borrow and result in higher interest rates on any new credit that you do obtain. But it can also cause interest rates on existing credit lines to rise as well (current lenders DO monitor your credit!).

Carrying too much debt can also cause you to go without a significant type of insurance coverage. It is another common way people deal with financial difficulties. It is a major reason why people go without medical insurance and probably the single leading cause they go without life insurance.

While not having those policies does save money in the short run, it can set a person or family up for a certified financial disaster in the future. The ultimate result of not having the coverage is a financial situation that is far worse than the initial financial struggle.

No one wants to think about debt—much less talk about it. And when it comes to actually doing something to get out of it, it's a challenge. You would certainly not be alone if you found yourself pretending to live in a unicorn-filled land where your student loan balance doesn't exist.

But as hard as it is to talk about, none of us are doing ourselves any favors if we can't be honest about the amount of debt being carried. If you think you might be guilty of spending too much time in a fantasy world, take our quiz to see if you're ready for a little reality.

How much of your money is yours and how much you pay toward your debt has a lot to do with how your debt got there in the first place.

There are several reasons for our debt accumulation, like paying for unforeseen emergencies or experiencing unemployment. But most often, our debt results from poor spending habits because unless you're spending cash, it's costing you money to spend money.

There are bullies behind our debt woes. There is a two-part accountability in debt creation. We have to take personal control of our own spending, but the lenders also have a form of impersonal control that can help or hinder us.

Imagine a credit card is someone granting you a favor to buy something you can't afford now but can easily pay off in the future. Well, the reality is that you simply end up owing more and owning less. We have been talking about the Joneses—those neighbors with the life and stuff we want—for almost 100 years and we still can't keep up with them. Unfortunately, never being content with what we have can lead to large amounts of debt.

Lacking the knowledge we need to manage that debt can keep those credit card balances static, or worse, allow them to grow.

Here's how. Imagine making a credit card purchase for $500. You rationalize spending the money because you look at it in $15 payments that are completely manageable. But what you don't see is the lender standing next to you with an outstretched hand wanting an additional $147 in interest charges.

At $15 per month, it would take you three and a half years to pay off the new $500 item at the average 2020 interest rate of 14.7 percent.

Considering that many credit cards have higher interest rates, this same purchase at 22 percent, for example, means handing over an additional $280 to the credit card company. Sure, you'll have four whole years to pay the $780, but will the item seem worth it when you finally own it outright?

When we add the small "wants" of our lives to the larger investments of financed homes and cars, and the planned "musts," such as college costs, weddings, unplanned medical emergencies, unemployment, and possible relocation, it's easy to see how debt grows.

Your monthly income should be dedicated to future planning, present comforts, and money for savings to reach goals and achieve whatever amount of financial security you desire.

Finally, individuals with good credit histories can borrow at lower interest rates because they are less of a risk for defaulting. Those with bad credit will get loans at considerably higher interest rates. They get a bigger hole of debt and have an increasingly smaller shovel of resources for filling it up.

But having good credit can be a detriment. If a lender sees you as a low-risk borrower because you have good credit, you could be more of a target for low-interest offers on lines of credit.

Evaluate You Decisions:

1. Do you stress about money but never make any changes?
YES_____   NO_____

2. Are you racking up other damaging behaviors?
YES_____   NO_____

3. Have you transferred your credit card balance more than once?
YES_____   NO_____

4. Do you fight with your partner or friends about money?
YES_____   NO_____

5. Do you ignore your bills?
YES_____   NO_____

6. Do you think your debt is "good" debt?

YES_____   NO_____

7. Are you totally focused on making more money to handle your debts?

YES_____   NO_____

How many of these did you answer "YES" to? One? Two? Seven?

If you identify yourself in even one of these, do these two things right now:

1. Pat yourself on the back for taking the first step toward ending your debt denial. Identifying the problem is the first step, according to just about every expert.

2. Make a commitment to be honest with yourself about your financial situation.

Chapter Four

Am I A Victim or Hopeless?

Another reason people have a poverty mindset is that they continue to think they're a victim of other people's choices and decisions. It's almost a blame game.

I'm going to openly discuss several signs of a poverty mentality that I hope you are moving away from or finding direction. Wealth creation can be greatly hindered by the smallest of things. Many are signs we cannot see for ourselves even when they are present. They are the things we get from society or our upbringing.

Many of these signs are assigning negative motives to people who are more prosperous than we are and finding ourselves jealous of what more successful people have, feeling like a powerless victim.

To my disbelief, some people find themselves celebrating the rich and famous then create massive amounts of debt trying to simulate things of the people they carry negative vibes towards.

I talked about this in other areas—*Maxing Out Your Income* and *Carrying Too Much Debt*—living above their means with out-of-control spending and debt accumulation.

Am I A Victim or Hopeless?

As a victim, they have to live out that role. They must speak negatively and they cannot allow themselves to dare to think they play a role in the hardship they are experiencing.

It's really hard to explain **"WHY"** it's easier to focus on how much money they lack rather than on how much money they can manifest. It does not help that much of their conversation with their poverty circle of friends is all about feeding a hatred or jealousy towards rich people.

Victims often want to escape from the reality of their poor decisions with money. This escape can be an irresistible trigger to blow away any savings or money earned from hard back-breaking work. This attempt to get away from reality may not have a very serious consequence at the moment, and won't be felt until months down the road.

Oftentimes, the person may feel the need to break away from life's daily grind and indulge in some form of pleasure like those they blame occasionally. This is not harmful in moderation.

However, that "I owe this to myself" mentality or the "I deserve this" thinking is a setup for a reality worse than before.

Due to the lack of financial knowledge, so many people find themselves in a state of hopelessness, the complete opposite of an escape from reality.

While an escapist holds on to the hope of better things (whether true or imaginary) that suits his or her wishes, the hopeless lose all sense of drive, the desire to move on, and even their imagination.

While we all have a tendency to feel hopeless at some point in our lives for various reasons, most of us can still think clearly with help from good advice and time to think. But when hopelessness treads the line towards desperation, there is a fragile spot where one could throw away everything that represents hard work over the years.

In all my years of working around money and assets, I have never found an occasion to consider money as an enemy. But there are those who for most of their life have related to money as an enemy.

They have always viewed finances as a necessary evil, a barrier that had to somehow be overcome in order to live a life free from worry. There are people who wish they had more money, and there are the hopeless who wish that money did not exist at all.

Believe it or not, people spend like money is the enemy, especially when they do not have it in unlimited supply. Hopelessness may be hovering over a serious or delicate issue and professional help or intervention may be in order. Do not laugh, this could be you. Think about it.

Every month there is a struggle to pay the minimum on your credit card bill and the balance keeps getting higher and higher. But you're still plopping that card down on the counter each morning at your local coffee shop.

Worse still, you know the card number by heart, so you don't even have to pull out your wallet when you make another online purchase.

Every time you think about your bank account, you suddenly have a cigarette in your hand. Or a donut. Or another beer. Or you're scrolling through some social media account for the 40th time that day.

Many of us from all over the world and from all walks of life, are having to deal with financial stress and uncertainty during this difficult time. Whether your problems stem from a loss of work, escalating debt, unexpected expenses, or a combination of factors, financial worry is one of the most common stressors in modern life.

Even before the global coronavirus pandemic and the resulting economic fallout, many were feeling stressed about money at least some of the time. Due to the recent economic difficulties, even more of us are now facing financial struggles and hardship.

Like any source of overwhelming stress, financial problems can take a huge toll on your mental and physical health, your relationships, and your overall quality of life.

Feeling beaten down by money worries can adversely impact your sleep, self-esteem, and energy levels.

It can leave you feeling angry, ashamed, or fearful, fuel tension and arguments with those closest to you, exacerbate pain and mood swings, and even increase your risk of depression and anxiety. You may resort to unhealthy coping mechanisms, such as drinking, abusing drugs, or gambling to try to escape your worries.

In the worst circumstances, financial stress can even prompt suicidal thoughts or actions. But no matter how hopeless your situation seems, there is help available. By tackling your money problems head on, you can find a way through the financial quagmire, ease your stress levels, and regain control of your finances—and your life.

While we all know that deep down there are many more important things in life than money, when you're struggling financially, fear and stress can take over your world. It can damage your self-esteem, make you feel flawed, and fill you with a sense of despair. When financial stress becomes overwhelming, your mind, body, and social life can pay a heavy price.

Numbing the pain with food and substances—even the internet—is classic avoidance behavior. Unfortunately, it's also a great way to pile problems on top of problems. After all, donuts aren't free.

So many people are on a constant hunt for another zero-percent-interest credit card to add to their arsenal. Transferring a balance to a card with no interest rate and engaging in a methodical plan to pay that balance off could be a smart financial choice. But it's not a long-term strategy. If you're trading credit card balances like baseball cards, you have a problem.

You need two hands to count the number of arguments you and your spouse have had about money in the last week. Every bill that crosses your door is cause for a serious row. If money is a constant source of discord with loved ones, it may be time to take a closer look at your financial health.

Imagine life without a student loan payment...

You throw your bills in a pile on your counter and hope they'll resolve themselves. When you do glance at them, it's only because you're moving them from one pile to another.

You're carrying a five-digit student loan balance, but you don't worry about paying it off because it's educational. It's good debt. Is it really?

Sure, people with college degrees get higher-paying jobs on average. And yes, student loan debt can actually boost your credit score in some cases. But graduates with high student loan balances may have less job flexibility, more stress over money, and more difficulty adjusting to a sudden financial change. None of that seems "good."

Unfortunately for all of us, bills rarely pay themselves. Sure, we've all seen an online meme about a good Samaritan who pays it forward, but they're probably not going to find the student loan bill you have shoved between a Pottery Barn catalog and a reminder for your next dental cleaning.

You keep telling yourself that the debt will be resolved if you could just get this next raise. Unfortunately, people have been saying that for years—and have gotten three raises. It's never enough. Your debt is still skyrocketing.

Of course, more money could be used to pay down more debt, but if that's not how you're spending the money you make, no raise or bonus will bring you financial freedom. This is a mindset that has nothing to do with money. It is you.

Not only is talking face-to-face with a trusted friend or loved one a proven means of stress relief, but speaking openly about your financial problems can also help you put things in perspective.

Keeping money worries to yourself only amplifies them until they seem insurmountable. The simple act of expressing your problems with someone you trust can make things seem far less intimidating.

The person you talk to doesn't have to be able to fix your problems or offer financial help. To ease your burden, they just need to be willing to talk things out without judging or criticizing.

Be honest about what you're going through and the emotions you're experiencing. Talking over your worries can help you make sense of what you're facing and your friend or loved one may even be able to come up with solutions that you hadn't thought of alone.

If you are feeling suicidal now…

Your money problems may seem overwhelming and permanent right now. But with time, things will get better and your outlook will change, especially if you get help. There are many people who want to support you during this difficult time, so please reach out!

Are You Feeling Suicidal? Call **1-800-273-TALK** in the U.S. or find a helpline at Suicide.org.

Chapter Five

The Breaking Point

The breaking point really pushes the can down the road for many, or does it? See, when someone has reached the breaking point, they have so many problems or difficulties that they can no longer cope with them and may soon collapse or be unable to continue. At the point at which a person gives way under stress, their situation becomes critical.

It is when people lose control. But "WHY?" What causes people to lose control financially? First of all, let me be clear on what I am about to say. When we think about being under financial stress or reaching a point of spending with no consciousness, one could think that we are only talking about the poor and uneducated.

As I talk about this group of people losing their spending control despite the fact that they may have good money management education, recognize how hard it is to save and how important it is to secure a good future.

These people (and that may include you and me) are coming from an all-too-human tendency to "misrepresent" **the good intentions** they have in few and far between financial splurges, expressed with a misinterpretation of money views.

Get this, people do the same thing or exhibit the same attitude for various reasons when it comes down to it. The same is true when one drastically overspends to the tune of a lifetime's worth of savings.

One of the unintended consequences of the evolution of our cultural values is the ability to secure instant gratification. We all want our desires met right away and now so many of these desires can actually be met immediately, but at a cost.

It is with this mindset that people lose all practical sense and become willing to throw away money, savings, and a financial future in one swift moment of happiness and fun.

It is said, there are many reasons for overspending and most of them are understandable, meaning they arise from a situation that may warrant action.

The issue boils down to how to manage impulsive spending triggers. A common thread among these impulsive behaviors is the so-called "breaking point," when one reaches the weakest point of the willpower and just simply "lets go."

Overspending is a bad habit and is one of the best ways to end up in a challenging financial position. No matter how hard it is, break these habits and set new goals to achieve. It is key to reaching financial independence and flying far away from debt.

Overspending is a disease and may be one of the reasons people have not achieved most of their goals.

However, like every disease has a cure, so does overspending. In order to solve such a disease, it is essential to get to the root of the problem: the causes and mindset.

Going from financial problems to a healthy financial status often requires organization and a shift in thinking. Avoiding overspending, building your savings, and gaining financial independence can often be accomplished with good spending habits.

The first thing you may want to try is creating a budget. There are many templates and resources available to help you create one. Sticking to one can be challenging, but simply having a budget laid out can help you see where you need to start spending less.

In addition to your budget, create a savings plan. Start out small. Even stowing away an extra dollar or two here and there can make a big difference. Also, try placing your savings in a place you cannot easily access. For example, create a savings account at a bank you don't usually use. The more difficult it is to access your money, the less likely you are to spend it.

Although the explanation of this part is the simplest, this is often the most challenging part to execute. It requires self-discipline and perseverance.

The most important part of this step is to know that if your plan doesn't work or if you have a difficult time sticking to it, all is not lost. If it happens, move on to the next step, evaluate your plan, and then repeat the process.

Overcoming financial obstacles can require changing your lifestyle and this does not happen overnight. However, just having a plan can help give confidence and reassurance that you can eventually overcome whatever is in your way.

Let's be honest, personal financial obstacles could come from many things: a lost job, a divorce, bankruptcy, a sudden medical emergency, or any situation in which your financial security crumbles beneath you. It's not always overspending and mismanagement.

Regardless of the cause, the consequences are often similar: emotional stress, confusion, perceived loss of control, and loss of confidence.

In the next two chapters, we are going to talk about the wisdom and confidence needed as you are enduring a financial crisis. Although it may be challenging, know that you can regain your financial stability once again. Your situation can be remedied by regaining your composure and taking concrete action.

I hate to say this but you need to be aware that negative emotions are normal. Before addressing the financial elements of a personal financial crisis, it is important to address the emotional elements as mentioned earlier. You have to recognize that emotional turmoil is a normal component of the process.

Depending on the cause of your situation, you may experience stress, depression, or anxiety. This may be accompanied by a sense of guilt or failure. You may also feel as if you have no control over your situation.

These emotions are a normal component of going through a financial crisis. While it may be difficult at first, these emotions will likely pass over time as you adjust to your new circumstances and regain control of the situation by taking action.

- Focus on being grateful for what you do currently have.
- Focus on accepting your financial situation.

When faced with a difficult situation, people often try to deny or ignore the situation. While it may feel better to do this, it does not help in the long run.

- Accepting your situation can empower you to face your difficulties as they are and conquer them head-on.
- Accepting the situation is the first step to resolving it.

Try to channel any negative energy about the situation into positive, solution-focused actions. For example, instead of dwelling on or blaming yourself for a scenario, try taking that negative energy and using it to make a commitment to solve the situation once and for all.

Talk about your situation. Confide in close friends or family members to talk out your worries and work out possible solutions aloud. Your confidant or accountability partner may be able to offer advice from their own experiences or from those of their friends.

Not only does this provide emotional support, but it exposes you to different and potentially more productive ways of approaching and dealing with the situation.

Commit to staying positive. Before making a plan to remedy your situation, make a commitment to focus on the positive.

Think about it this way: While the cause of your situation may not be in your control, how you choose to react to it is. Thinking positively can improve your mood, reduce your stress, and help you approach the situation in a way that is conducive to solving it.

Remember that regardless of your situation, others have faced and solved it before.

This can be your breaking point. In order to motivate yourself to get out of this crisis, you'll have to remind yourself **WHY** you want to improve your situation.

In other words, what will you be unable to do because of your current situation? Be realistic about your life goals and calculate the costs of achieving those goals.

Think about how sitting back and settling into your new financial situation will hurt you and those around you in the long run.

Your recovery plan will have to remedy the problem that got you into the financial crisis in the first place. Put simply, you will have to reduce debt if you have it and earn more income to replace your lost assets and financial security.

This may mean getting a new job, getting an additional job, cutting your expenses, applying for government assistance, or seeking debt forgiveness.

The simplest way to dig yourself out of debt and live sustainably off of your income is to reduce expenses and increase your income.

Options like bankruptcy, while necessary in some cases, can also ruin your credit and cause a large amount of hassle.

The Breaking Point

How well does this statement describe you or your situation?

1. I could handle a major unexpected expense.

This statement describes me

Completely   Very well   Somewhat   Very little   Not at all

2. I am securing my financial future.

This statement describes me

Completely   Very well   Somewhat   Very little   Not at all

3. Because of my money situation, I feel like I will never have the things I want in life.

This statement describes me

Completely   Very well   Somewhat   Very little   Not at all

4. I can enjoy life because of the way I'm managing my money.

This statement describes me

Completely   Very well   Somewhat   Very little   Not at all

5. I am just getting by financially.

This statement describes me

Completely   Very well   Somewhat   Very little   Not at all

6. I am concerned that the money I have or will save won't last.

This statement describes me

Completely   Very well   Somewhat   Very little   Not at all

46

Chapter Six

Wisdom is a Shelter

Have you ever spent your money on an urge? What made you decide to succumb to that wanton spending urge? What would you change if you had the chance?

By identifying "deadly" money views that could prove fatal to your future security and understanding what triggers them, you can save yourself a lot of regret and spare your loved ones the burden of dealing with your money mismanagement.

Because our topic involves personal attitude, life views, and mindsets in relation to how we look at and use money, we will be dealing with life skills on proper money views and its application to decision-making.

Hence, we won't be tackling functional skills on managing your finances such as making a weekly or a monthly budget or balancing your income and spending.

However, we will give practical guides on how to fight off the irrational urge to spend your savings which you can use as preparatory steps to develop money-life skills for wealth creation.

I want to speak straight to the hearts and minds of all readers needing to re-examine their views about money and their life in general.

I'm speaking to the heart because our financial management discussion involves strong and personal emotions. I'm talking to the mind because it requires self-control, understanding, and open-mindedness to live a life of security and happiness founded on a healthy, prudent, and realistic view of money.

I trust that these approaches to sensible financial management and spending suggestions will gear people up who are seeking wealth creation.

I want people who are committed to sticking to a savings plan for the long-term, but find their savings duty waning or tiring, to be reawakened and their savings zeal reenergized.

I want you to resolve to hang on to your money and life goals no matter what, so that you may be further encouraged to continue by being reminded of the more meaningful reasons why you are saving faithfully in the first place.

You must want and need more concrete personal financial management. You can do this by learning the life skills of self-affirmation and spending control and developing healthy money views and better life perspectives. Ultimately, you must apply these mindsets to your daily lives.

This is aimed to help change the way you look at money in relation to your happiness and well-being, change some attitudes and mindsets that hinder your aspiration for long-term security, stick to your already good spending lifestyle, or make improvements.

The previous chapters were all about "deadly" money views that have been fatal to financial security. Before we talk about the millionaire mindset and the wealth mindset, we must understand they share similarities and differences.

You can save yourself a lot of regrets and spare your loved ones the burden of dealing with your money mismanagement when you recognize what triggers your deadly money views.

Stop, look at every adversity (failure) carefully, analyze it, and look for what might be good in it. You may be surprised. It could be that what you thought was a problem is actually an opportunity.

A wisdom mindset requires you to make a habit of looking for the good in your financial life. When you make a habit of looking for the good, there's a good chance you will find it. Another way of saying this is, "Every cloud has a silver lining."

Every adversity brings with it the **seeds of an equivalent advantage.** The very same interest that compounds on credit card debt can do so on investments.

Instead of paying banking fees, try carrying and meeting the average daily balance and get free perks. What were over the limit fees, low balance fees, late fees, and monthly fees could be used to buy stocks that pay dividends.

Setbacks happen to us all so we need to keep this in mind: The more we reach and the more chances we take, the more setbacks we will encounter. It's across the board—whether it's love, war, or business, we will always encounter setbacks. Financial setbacks are no different.

When we do experience setbacks, it's good to refer to the wisdom that's there to guide us—the wisdom we can apply to help us bounce back. Sometimes we can think, "Woe is me! They've cut back my income 15%!" or "I can't find another job!" While that's not good, it could be tough, and it could be true, there are ways that we can always make things work.

I like to be an innovator at times and come up with new ways to help people move from a poverty (fixed) mindset to a wealth creation (growth) mindset. When they are taking one of my courses, they are so eager to pass. When they don't pass a course, they get the grade, "Not Yet."

To me, this is a fantastic way of not showing them their failure because when most people get a failing score, they think, *I'm nothing, and I'm going nowhere.* **But if they get the grade, "Not Yet," they understand that they're on a learning curve. It gives them a path into the future**.

"Not Yet" can also give early insight into a critical event that becomes a real turning point.

I wanted to see how my investment club partners coped with challenge and difficulty, so I gave them investment problems that were slightly too hard for most of them. Shockingly, some of them reacted in a positive way.

They said things like, "I love a challenge," or, "You know, I was hoping this would be informative." They understood that their abilities could be developed. They had what is called a growth mindset.

Others felt it was tragic and catastrophic. From their fixed mindset perspective, their intelligence had been up for judgment and they failed. Instead of luxuriating in the power of yet, they were gripped in the tyranny of now.

So, what did they do next? I'll tell you what they did next. Some told me they probably wouldn't take the course the next time, another group wanted to see someone who did worse than they did so they could feel better about themselves, and others said it was simply too difficult.

It's easy to fall into the trap of NOW. People become obsessed with winning—they dream of the action to prove themselves instead of dreaming big. A by-product of this is that people are becoming dependent on validation.

What can we do about this? Don't praise intelligence or talent, praise work ethic instead.

We can praise wisely, not praising intelligence or talent. That has failed. There are a lot of intelligent and talented broke, poverty mindset individuals out here. Do not do that anymore. Instead, **praise the process: the effort, the strategies, the focus, the perseverance, and the improvement. Praising the process creates individuals who are hardy and resilient**.

The way we word things affects confidence. The words "yet" or "not yet," gives greater confidence which gives a path into the future that creates greater persistence. We can change mindsets.

Every time you are pushed out of your comfort zone to learn something new and difficult, the neurons in your brain can form new, stronger connections. Over time, you can get smarter.

People who are not taught this growth mindset experience a continuous decline in financial matters, but those who are taught the lesson show a sharp rebound in dealing with challenging difficulty.

Shelter

Let's talk about the mindset. It is being confident in wisdom. There's a scripture from the Bible that comes to mind.

First, I am going to paraphrase it. It says, when the axe is dull it requires more strength, but wisdom will guide you to sharpen the blade.

How often do you find yourself working very hard at things, trying to accomplish what you know is meant for you to do?

Do you ever find yourself struggling in an area that you have great insight and great vision in, yet you find it difficult to process, proceed, or move forward?

A wisdom mindset will guide you to sharpen your blade so that more power or more strength is not necessary for you to complete the process.

The wisdom of sharpening the blade, eliminating the hardship, allows you to remove yourself from the position of stagnation so that you can continue your efforts towards moving forward.

Strange enough, most of us see money as a tool, but it's not. Money is a shelter. "Wisdom is a shelter as money is a shelter, but the advantage of knowledge is this: Wisdom preserves those who have it" (Ecclesiastes 7:12).

There are nearly 80+ references in the Bible that speak on "shelter," more than 200 references that speak on "wisdom," and over 2,300 that speak on "prosperity." There is a spiritual connection to wealth creation that impacts every single one of us.

A shelter is protection, a covering, a defense. This is what your money should provide you in every area of your life. Sometimes people become comfortable with money and wealth without understanding what is required of them. Protecting your wealth is just as important as growing it.

Your wealth creation depends on a variety of circumstances, some of which are uncontrollable. However, when you're prepared with a protection strategy the uncontrollable has the potential to become manageable.

Instating a strategy with guaranteed income and/or estate benefits can help protect your money (shelter) by leveraging your ability to give attention to the unforeseen.

You deserve to know that you matter and what you're striving for is achievable with disciplined, tactical strategies and a dedicated commitment to yourself and your future.

For me, writing this series is about more than just guiding you towards managing your wealth, it's being your constant pillar of sound advice throughout every stage of your life.

Your protection, your shelter, your covering, is all tied to you practicing discipline. When you do so, you're better equipped to help others in need or to treat those you love on special occasions.

Shelter

Financial discipline matters to your success even when wealth creation isn't your priority. Strong money habits facilitate being able to be successful on your own terms.

By consistently reminding yourself of your core goals and drawing a line between them and financial stability, you'll be motivated to stay disciplined and you will achieve the fulfilling life of which you've dreamed.

Chapter Seven

Confidence of Purpose

Most people never go beyond the wishing and wanting stages of life. It is no accident that the wealthiest people of society make up only 3%.

This 3% does something more than the larger group—they have the mindset to create and win. When you are in pursuit of wealth creation, every single act, every single moment should be about winning even when you lose.

It is about your "Confidence of Purpose." I want to discuss your confidence and building a mindset with a confident attitude. Having confidence and believing in yourself can take you further than you could possibly imagine in life.

Whatever your goal, being confident, keeping a clear and positive focus, and eliminating negativity, can mean the difference between success and failure. This is a basic and vitally important piece of the puzzle whenever you are seeking to make changes for the better.

You have to believe in yourself and your ability to attain your objective. In this case, creating and building wealth is the primary purpose. Yes, I know some people seem to be born with a lot of confidence. For the rest of us, confidence is built over time through our attitudes, our past experiences, and our relationship to the world.

Confidence of Purpose

Let me be clear, when I say confidence, I don't just mean the general state of being confident around others. I am referring to being confident in the fact that you and your life have a purpose. If you maintain a positive attitude, live life to the fullest, and treat others with dignity and respect, you are already demonstrating both purpose and confidence.

If you view your money and financial situation with a positive attitude, manage it to the fullest, and treat money with respect and dignity, you will discover both confidence and purpose.

Sometimes, it seems difficult to develop a confident and positive mindset with money. This is especially true if you have had many financial challenges. No matter what your income level is, there could be difficulty. One thing I believe you can do is to make a list of all the things you are good at with money. This could be anything from tracking your spending to paying your bills on time.

Write absolutely everything down no matter how small. It all counts. Next, add any achievements you've managed to attain over the course of your life so far, even if it's a simple action where you paid off a bill or opened a savings account. Look over this list and feel proud because you should be. Continue to add to this list over time, as you continue to achieve successes.

Other Ways to Develop Confidence:

• **Speak Up**. Often, we don't speak up because we're afraid that others will judge us for saying something stupid. There are no stupid statements or questions when seeking knowledge. Generally, people are much more accepting than you think. Moreover, others are often dealing with the exact same fears. Make an effort to speak up in group situations. You'll develop more confidence in your ideas and improve your wealth creation skills.

• **Make an effort to look your best**. When you look your best, it changes the way you carry yourself and the way you interact with others. When you dress well and pay attention to your grooming, it affects how you feel about yourself. Making an effort to look your best automatically gives you more confidence. Most importantly, in makes it easier to attract like minds.

• **Work out**. The many benefits of physical fitness are too numerous to go into at length here. Bottom line: Being in shape gives you more confidence in yourself, your abilities, and your energy, and improves your mood and mental capabilities. It's all good news. It even increases your energy towards the pursuit of wealth.

• **Focus on contribution**. The more you contribute to the community the better you'll feel about yourself. An added bonus is that contributions are often rewarded with more personal success and recognition. In turn, these increase your feelings of self-confidence.

- **Practice good posture.** The way you carry yourself tells everyone how you feel about yourself. Practicing good posture automatically helps you feel more confident. Stand up straight, keep your head up, and make eye contact. You'll make a positive impression on others and instantly feel more alert and empowered.

Building confidence and having a positive attitude is crucial when it comes to reaching goals. We all want abundance in life. Whether it's with our families or at work, we all want to be successful. The secret key to unlocking your happiness and success is learning how to be more positive in every sense of the word.

The truth is, your happiness and success lie within your own hands. Always believe in yourself and your unique value. In the end, having self-confidence and a positive attitude is an inside job. That's good news because you're in charge of what goes on in your mind and feelings.

Henry Ford said: "Whether you think you can, or you think you can't—you're right." Wise Words.

There are two main mindsets we can navigate life with: growth or fixed. Having a growth mindset is essential for success.

We succeed (or not) based on what is within our control to foster success. The two mindsets and the difference they make in outcomes are incredibly powerful.

You have to examine the self-conceptions (or mindsets) you use to structure yourself and guide behavior. These mindsets play a role in motivation and self-regulation, and they impact achievement and interpersonal processes.

There are consequences to thinking that your intelligence or personality is something you can develop as opposed to something that is a fixed, deep-seated trait.

Your view of yourself determines everything. If you believe that your qualities are unchangeable—the fixed mindset—you will want to prove yourself correct over and over rather than learn from your mistakes.

If you have only a certain amount of intelligence, a certain personality, and a certain moral character, then you'd better prove that you have a healthy dose of them. It simply wouldn't do any good to look or feel deficient in these most basic characteristics.

I've seen so many people with the one goal of proving themselves—in the classroom, in their careers, and in their relationships. Every situation calls for a confirmation of their intelligence, personality, or character. I used to be this way without recognizing that I had a fixed mindset. For me, every situation was evaluated: Will I succeed or fail? Will I look smart or dumb? Will I be accepted or rejected? Will I feel like a winner or a loser?

People struggle financially because of the fixed mindset. They seem to know it all and refuse to accept advice that is different from their thinking. People can grow up in the same city, with the same parents, attend the same school, and still have dissimilar financial traits.

Intelligence, personality, and character are culturally desirable. We value these traits and it's normal to want them.

59

But…

There's another mindset in which these traits are not simply the hand you're dealt. With this mindset, you're always trying to convince yourself and others that you have a royal flush when you're secretly worried it's a pair of tens.

With this mindset, the hand you're dealt is just the starting point for development. This is the growth mindset. It is based on the belief that your basic qualities are things you can cultivate through your efforts. Changing your beliefs can have a powerful impact. The growth mindset creates a powerful passion for learning. Why waste time proving over and over how great you are when you could be getting better?

Why hide deficiencies instead of overcoming them? Why look for friends or partners who will just shore up your self-esteem instead of ones who will also challenge you to grow? Why seek out the tried and true, instead of experiences that will stretch you?

The passion for stretching yourself and sticking to it, even (or especially) when it's not going well, is the hallmark of the growth mindset. This is the mindset that allows people to thrive during some of the most challenging times in their lives.

Our ideas about risk and effort come from our mindset. Some people realize the value of challenging themselves. They want to put in the effort to learn and grow. Others, however, would rather avoid the effort. They feel like it doesn't matter.

We often see self-help books crowding the shelves of bookstores and these books may give many useful tips. But they're usually a list of unconnected pointers, like "You too can be rich;" "Good morning, Millionaire;" or "Believe in yourself."

While you're left admiring people who can do that, it's never clear how these things fit together or how you could ever become that way. You're inspired for a few days, but basically, the world's most successful people still have their secrets. I pray that my work here will not leave you in such a state of mind. No sugarcoating here.

Instead, as you begin to understand the fixed and growth mindsets, you will see exactly how one thing leads to another—how a belief that your qualities are carved in stone leads to a host of thoughts and actions, and how a belief that your qualities can be cultivated leads to a host of different thoughts and actions, taking you down the road of "Wealth Creation."

Sure, people with the fixed mindset have read the books that say: Success is about being your best self, not about being better than others; Failure is an opportunity, not a condemnation; and Effort is the key to success.

But they can't put this into practice because their basic mindset—their belief in fixed traits—is telling them something entirely different: Success is about being more gifted than others; Failure does measure you; and Effort is for those who can't make it on talent. Or, "I can't save money right now, I will when I get a raise. I am okay where I am."

This fixed mindset is the twin brother to the poverty mindset which says, "I don't have to own a house when I can rent one."

Exceptional people seem to have a special talent for converting life's setbacks into future successes. There is wide agreement about the number one ingredient in creative achievement. It is exactly the kind of perseverance and resilience produced by the growth mindset.

With a growth mindset, failure can be a painful experience but it doesn't define you. It's a problem to be faced, dealt with, and learned from. We can still learn from our mistakes. You're not a failure until you start to assign blame. You stop learning from your mistakes when you deny them.

Wealth creation will have moments of failure and moments of disappointment, but you must not allow those moments to defeat you. As I stated earlier, debt problems, mental health problems, and income problems are directly tied to having a different mindset.

Chapter Eight

Personality & Character Ethics

As I try to get you to explore the mindset, there must be a consideration of Personality Ethic and Character Ethic. Even with money, there is a form of ethics that has an impact on the day-to-day.

As I began creating the content for this series, I reflected on my past pain. Because of what I have seen in the lives of people I have worked with over the years, I began to feel that much of the success I helped people achieve was superficial. It was filled with social image consciousness and techniques for a quick fix: Get out of debt, improve your credit score, and create a budget.

Reluctantly, I feel that I only addressed minimum problems and sometimes even appeared to solve them temporarily, leaving the underlying chronic problem untouched to fester and reappear time and time again. "WHY?" I never once dealt with the mindset itself, the foundation of Character Ethic.

The foundation of this mindset deals with positive traits like integrity, humility, fidelity, temperance, courage, justice, patience, industry, simplicity, modesty, and the golden rule. It is essentially the effort to integrate certain principles and habits deep within the nature of the mindset, Character Ethic.

There are basic principles of effective living that people only experience through success and enduring happiness as they learn and integrate these principles into the mindset.

Personality & Character Ethics

Personality Ethic success becomes a function of personality as the public image of attitudes, behavior, skills, and techniques lubricate the process of human interaction.

Personality Ethic essentially takes two paths: One is a human and public relations technique and the other is a positive mental attitude. Your attitude determines your altitude, smiling wins more friends than frowning, and whatever the mind of the man can conceive and believe it can achieve.

I believe that most people often feel like they want to do something different but they are unsure of how to go about it. And let's be real, most times it's because they are afraid of change. When you involve money in this conversation it complicates matters even more.

Developing a growth mindset is one way to create excitement in your life and change the patterns you might be stuck in. I challenge you to challenge yourself to create the best life possible for you.

I am convinced that if developing a new mindset, simply dealing with Personality Ethic and Character Ethic will lead you to discover that money and wealth creation is truly a mindset.

There are many books on personal development. One of my favorites is "Walden or Life in the Woods" by Henry David Thoreau. Its contents (advice on simple living and self-sufficiency leading to personal growth) are still relevant today. Mind you, this book was written in the 1800s, over 200 years ago. People have been constantly in pursuit of improving their mindset.

I hope you will discover that our character is deeper and more complex than our visible personality. Look at it this way, our personality is the bit above the water. It's what we present to the world.

This includes what we say and do, how we dress, how we present ourselves, and how we interact with others. To some extent, our personality is shallow. It can be a bit of an act that is disconnected from our core selves.

Now when we consider our character, it is below the water. This part of us is comprised of our principles, beliefs, and motivations. If only we could dwell in this space daily. It encompasses traits like integrity, fidelity, courage, compassion, contribution, responsibility, and justice. Our personal values are a reflection of the true beliefs that shape our character.

This brings us to Character Ethic vs. Personality Ethic. Character Ethic vs. Personality Ethic is determined by each individual person but can also be influenced by societal norms and expectations.

Character Ethic focuses on foundational traits, including integrity, humility, hard work, loyalty, self-control, courage, justice, patience, modesty, and morality. These are basic principles that any person in any culture or time period could agree are important.

Personality Ethic emphasizes skills and practices that affect your public image, attitudes, and behaviors. This approach offers quick-fix solutions—how to be more charming, have a more positive outlook, make people like you, and influence people to do what you want.

However, these solutions generally only work temporarily, while the underlying problem remains and ultimately resurfaces.

Character Ethic vs. Personality Ethic can be broken down this way: Character Ethic addresses primary traits, while Personality Ethic addresses secondary traits, like communication skills, interpersonal strategies, and positive thinking.

These techniques are often essential for success, but they are flimsy and ineffective if they're not based on the character that supports them. You must start with the foundation.

For example, if you try to use communication skills to make people trust you but your character is not honest and trustworthy, the effects will be hollow and eventually people will see through the act.

Wealth Creation, managing money, and investing all rely on character traits, or should I say, ethics. Your strategy will not be effective simply because people might like you and you are charming. Real results will occur when you sincerely apply Character Ethic.

You can also think of Character Ethic vs. Personality Ethic this way: In one-time or short-term scenarios, you may be able to get by on personality alone.

But without the foundation of primary traits—Character Ethic—the secondary traits will never have a lasting impact.

Working on personality improvements without first establishing the necessary character traits would be like a farmer trying to fit all their work into one season.

If the farmer skips planting in the spring, neglects to water and nurture the buds all summer, then tries to plant, water, and harvest in the fall, it won't work.

You can't shortcut the process, and you can't ignore the differences between Character Ethic vs. Personality Ethic when you need both to change your mindset.

Character Ethic vs. Personality Ethic is an important distinction. They both create the foundation you need to be effective. You need to understand this part of yourself in order to seek changing your mindset.

Poverty Mindset vs. Wealth Mindset carries an identical process to wealth creation. Poverty mindset constantly gives someone many one-time or short-term scenarios that bring minimum results.

For example, you receive a large tax return and place that money in a savings account. Not long afterwards, you are withdrawing the money to do things that make you feel good, look good, or to impress others.

Luxury homes, fancy cars, morning attitudes of affirmation (Good morning, Millionaire), social events, grinding—the list of traits that represent Personality Ethic is so long. There is no value, no hard work, no self-control, and no integrity. All of the foundational traits are without purpose.

Now I am making this personal to you—at least I hope that I am. Please know that there is an important difference between values and ethics. I believe the distinction is incredibly helpful in your understanding of finances.

Ethics is defined as a system of moral principles. Ethics deals with right and wrong. Values is defined as relative worth, merit, or importance. Values deals with what is important to a given person.

Hypothetically, if we were all getting our ethics from the same source, they would not change from one person to another—what is right or wrong for you, would also be right or wrong for me.

Values, on the other hand, could vary significantly from one person to another. You may value security; I may value freedom. One person might value hospitality, another person might value travel, while someone else values compassion. Some people may value homeownership while others value renting.

None of those values are inherently right or wrong, they are just different. Each person simply places more worth (or value) on one than the other.

The difference between ethics and values prompts a unique question in my mind—one that I've been wrestling with for quite some time.

What is the role that ethics should play in my personal finances?

What is right and what is wrong in how one pursues, accumulates, and spends money?

It seems that most people have a broad definition that they use to answer those questions. We apply broad ethics to our finances.

Things like:

- It is wrong to steal money.
- It is wrong to extort money.
- It is wrong to bribe with money.

- It is wrong to be jealous of others.
- It is moral and right for me to help others financially when I am able to do so.

These are financial ethics that most of us adhere to in our lives and our pursuit, accumulation, and spending of money.

So, we routinely apply ethics to our finances—but only broadly. Beyond that broad application, we don't tend to get detailed in our pursuit of financial ethics. Instead, we tend to make our everyday financial decisions based on values rather than ethics. This creates a clear distinction between poverty creation and wealth creation.

We do not ask detailed questions that sound like this:

- Is it wrong for me to spend this much money on a car?
- Is it wrong for me to buy this size of house?
- What is my moral obligation to pay off debt rather than spend on myself?
- Is it okay for me to make this much money?
- What is an ethical amount of money I should be saving this month?
- What is an ethical amount of money I should give to help others?
- Is there a moral question to be asked in how much (or how little) I am paying for this service?

Most of us, more often than I'd like to admit, do not ask those ethical questions of our everyday financial decisions, myself included. Instead, we base our decisions on values:

- I want x, and I have the money to buy x, so I am going to buy it.
- This is important to me, so I am going to spend money on it.
- My goal is to have this much money in the bank, so I am going to keep everything for myself until I reach that number.
- I want to make as much money as possible, and here's how I can do that.

You see how that works? Values guide our financial decisions, not ethics.

Except for one area...

When it comes to others, we are quick to apply a filter of financial ethics that we rarely ask of ourselves. As a financial coach, I will put filters on you.

This is particularly prevalent today in our opinions of those with more. We live in a society that is quick to identify those with more who are not applying ethics to their financial circumstances. In our opinion, they are not being guided by ethics.

So, we are quick to make moral judgments that they…

—should not have that much money.
—should not spend their money in that specific way.
—should not buy x.
—should spend more money on y.
—should be giving away more.
—shouldn't be driving that kind of car.
—shouldn't be living in a house that big (or owning that many houses).
—are selfish because they have z.

Because they are not spending their money in the way we believe they should be spending their money, they are greedy, selfish, or immoral.

Meanwhile, the person's financial ethics we should be most concerned about is our own. We are quick to place a filter of ethics on the decisions of others, but rarely apply those same filters to our own.

Indeed, ours is the only pocketbook and bank account we have control over. Rather than spending time concerning ourselves with others, we should focus intently on our own personal financial ethics and how to apply it to our unique financial circumstance.

After all, ours is the only pocketbook and bank account that we will have to give an account for at the end of our work lives.

Am I proud of how I pursued, accumulated, and spent my financial resources? This is a question that we will all face at the end of our work lives.

We can be proud knowing that we lived a life aligned with our values. But an even greater amount of pride can be found knowing we lived what was right, moral, and ethical. The person's financial ethics we should be most concerned about is our own—not anyone else's.

WEALTH CREATION
THE SERIES

MINDSET

The seed has been planted…

Now that you have read about various stages and types of mindsets, it is time to begin developing your new mindset.

Wealth Creation is a long game that requires very healthy financial habits and ethics. Most wealthy people have fully mastered the long game.

They have a clear understanding of their financial mission, vision, and purpose. More importantly, they take Action Influence steps every single day to maximize their chances of fulfilling their Wealth Creation goals.

There is a Magic Bullet for Wealth Creation…

…it's called Mechanics.

Do not read beyond this point if you will not take action!

Chapter Nine

Cultivating the Mindset

I trust that I did my part in causing you to begin to think about the quality of your mind long before you got to this chapter of the book. The quality of your mind (your mental) determines the quality of your life. This also applies to your financial life as well.

If your base, or foundation, always seems to draw inaccurate conclusions about who you are and what you're capable of doing, you will only limit your potential. It's like what I said in the last chapter about personality traits.

Now that you have been exposed to various quality traits that can guide you to greater accomplishment, let's get ready to grow.

The first stage is to lay the foundation for wealth creation, beginning with developing your strategy, habits, psychology, and mindset.

A lot of people try to create wealth by starting a business or by investing. Unfortunately, they forget about the inner game of success. Earlier, I mentioned a time when I gave my client and student just enough to be successful in the short-term. I want to share a story with you.

In week three of teaching one of my classes, a student spoke to me after class and told me that their spouse was afraid of money. They added that money seemed to always intimidate them. As I listened to their concerns, I remembered that one of my mentees had gone through something very similar. I decided to reach out to her and asked her to come and share her story.

She shared her story and the class enjoyed hearing it. Some students were actually able to find peace in their struggle.

The first thing she shared was the first task that I had given her. That first task was to read the book "The Slight Edge," by Jeff Olson. I assigned that task to challenge her mentally.

It was amazing to hear her share the impact that it had on her life.

She has since become a renowned speaker and author. She is a powerful source of information and strategies for businesses and individuals. She is Asia Kuykendall, the author of "Quantum Wealth Theory."

Quantum Wealth Theory is a weekly planner designed as a 12-step method to help jump start the process of understanding your relationship with money and customizing a road map to guide you on your journey.

Everyone's ideal version of wealth is uniquely different. It takes a certain mentality to recognize these unique ideals—a Wealth Mentality.

This Wealth Mentality starts with overcoming whatever mental, emotional, and societal barriers that keep you from building wealth. Through the guided missions, you learn to recognize the other forms of wealth that you have immediate access to.   Visit www.quantumwealththeory.com for more information.

If you believe that you want Wealth Creation, naturally you will do whatever it takes for Wealth Creation. However, if you have not yet done the work to reprogram your limits by setting them to your beliefs, you'll only end up sabotaging your process. It's the character ethics that produces the results.

Reprogramming starts the cultivation process of **purging**. It is often an essential method for maintaining healthy habits, preventing debt accumulation, and encouraging financial growth. Beware, it's possible to over cultivate, or purge, causing financial problems, preventing wealth growth, and creating problems in other areas as well.

After a harsh early start to managing money and dealing with debt, the time has come to start cultivating the mindset and preparing your wealth creation journey for the new season in your life.

- But when exactly should the cultivation begin?
- Is there an optimal time?

Wealth Creation mindset cultivation involves three vital steps that must be followed: purge, prepare, and be purposeful.

Step One: Purge

Purging involves breaking up bad relationships and turning away from everything on the surface or internally that has blocked you in some form.

This is a fundamental step, especially in the case of a mindset that has been compacted with limits or fear for several years. If your mindset is not purged of all the bad experiences and the negativity has not been removed, there is a high certainty that you will only cultivate your personality, and not reach the deeper layers of your character.

Often the effect of purging can be enhanced by building new relationships. This consists of attending events that will elevate you. You may have heard the saying that if your circle of friends is full of fives and sixes, it's simple to know that you are not a 10.

Today's culture often speaks of money/wealth as bags—a large sum of money obtained at once or accumulatively from a single activity. However, the value of the bag has diminished greatly, it's simply getting money by the hour.

Your mindset of how you see, think, and feel about money can no longer be negative in any way. People like to languish in a lack mentality, convinced that they'll never achieve wealth creation. They're constantly struggling to feel secure.

Step Two: Prepare

True cultivating is an inside job. Being a wealth creator begins with feeling ready to receive wealth. Whatever we think about money leads to how we feel about money.

You cannot operate in a lack/poverty mentality and expect to accumulate or create wealth.

You cannot believe that you will never have enough, that you will never be enough, or that there is too much lack in the world.

You cannot believe that when you have a lot of money, you're superior to others in some way, e.g., you're smarter or you work harder.

You cannot fear having money because you associate it with negative qualities.

You cannot have a story that says, "I don't want to be seen in that way."

You cannot place importance on money and see yourself as inferior if you don't have a certain amount.

You cannot fear having a lot of money and not enjoy it because you fear losing it.

You cannot believe having money makes you better or less than others.

I hope these "Cannots" have opened your mind to a point where you realize that you can get in your own way. Now, start to become very conscious. Throughout the day, pay attention to your thoughts and energy as well as your behavior around money.

Remember Character Ethic, your inside work. Realize that it too will come under attack as you commit to this new journey.

Some of the most powerful hits you will take will be false evidence appearing real to you. When you notice those fearful thoughts around money, use the moment to create a new thought about your new journey.

It's normal to become tempted. As you catch yourself staring into a boutique's window thinking, "I wish I could afford that great pair of boots" or "I really owe this to myself," remember the "Cannots."

That simple shift redirects your energy. This is when you must have gratitude and positivity. In an instant, you will remember that you are doing a great thing for yourself.

When you take away the need to look for lack and look for wealth creation instead, wealth creation becomes what you see. Your true success starts with your belief system, so choose to see through the lens of gratitude.

If you begin to regularly practice gratitude by taking time to notice and reflect on the things you are thankful for, you will experience positive emotions, feel more alive, sleep better, express more compassion and kindness, and have a stronger immune system. Yes, a stronger immune system. I believe that gratitude is one of the fuels to wealth creation.

Step Three: Be Purposeful

As a financial coach, I am often upset with many of my colleagues in this wealth creation space. Their initial discussions always seem to be about their diverse clients who are successful individuals or families, those who are near or in retirement, business owners, and corporate executives.

They make is seem as though these are the only individuals who are in pursuit of wealth creation. This one simple thought could put a burden of some sort on you. You must think and become purposeful with every step and action. This process is for you as well.

Earlier, I told you that there is a silver bullet to wealth creation, called "Mechanics." Yes, the mechanics of you being purposeful in your journey will change your life forever.

There must be a way to think purposefully about the major wealth creation decisions you must make. It is great that I have a chance to explain to you—in plain and simple English—the basics you must know in order to implement purposeful wealth creation.

I am writing this for every person who wants to make work optional and maintain that status. Purposeful wealth creation reveals a process for ascertaining your personal goals, values, needs, resources, and obligations, then purposefully orchestrating the five key elements of wealth management: investment, taxation, estate planning, insurance, and charitable intent.

There are two sides to every financial power story: the technical and the relational. You need to make the right decisions for financial growth and the right decisions for positive impact.

Accumulating and having wealth is a great responsibility and it should be managed with purpose. The benefits of wealth include financial security, the ability to spend time not earning an income, and a more comfortable lifestyle. There are a number of significant things that wealth is not able to secure including personal health, the joy of family, and contentment.

You create a purposeful wealth experience to address all aspects of your wealth. Wealth is useless if there is constant worry about money instead of contentment in the heart. It is also useless if there is no consideration of the long term impact.

My goal is that you understand that wealth alone does not accomplish anything. A holistic understanding must be achieved so that wealth can be used to its maximum potential.

I believe that as you manage wealth according to established wisdom principles, you will experience contentment under all economic conditions, confidence in your financial decisions, and excellent communication with everyone involved. This will result in maximized generosity of time, talents, and treasure.

Your financial goals, aspirations, and investment needs are just that—yours. Your financial purposes should reflect that.

Do not settle for an off-the-shelf investment program. I hope this book provides you with the ability to personalize your wealth creation based on your goals, your time frame, and your particular tolerance for risk.

I can write, speak, and coach in a way to provide you with the right combination of financial insight, support, and guidance that makes the most sense for you, but you must establish purpose.

Once you've established purpose, you can start moving forward in a very purposeful way. An equally important part of your purpose is tackling major issues you might not see coming, like a family or health-related event.

You must leave no stone unturned as you craft and build the big picture of your financial situation. Guide it towards its destination and look for ways improve.

Cultivating the Mindset

Without cultivating your mindset, money will be an area of resistance for you. It will trigger a lot of family wounds and old stories.

Our money mindset is often a direct reflection of however our family handled money or believed in money. It also reflects the collective consciousness and our life stories around money and wealth creation.

Cultivating the Mindset

You may have to heal your money mindset in order to begin to change. It is really about your energy. It will attract what you think and what you feel about practically everything.

Remember, energy is everything, even in your wallet. Energy is currency, so for the sake of your finances and wealth creation, clean up your wallet, clean up your mental financial files, and start to clear the energetic connection to your wealth creation.

If your wallet is beaten up, overstuffed, or if you just don't like it, clean it up or get a new one. Not only will your new, clean wallet energetically support you, but it will also make a statement to the Universe that you're ready to receive.

The information shared thus far is about you discovering your Character Ethic, which is normally dormant in most people, and creating a new mindset that will take you to a whole new dimension.

Remember, creating a habit helps our brain retain a pattern. The longer and more consistently you work to keep the habit, the better your brain will be at scanning the world for the positive.

You will be more successful if you can involve your family as you create new habits. Remember a positive brain is more creative, more productive, and more engaged. That's exactly what you want as you cultivate a new mindset.

I reached out to an author who is a personal friend of mine to get a few words from him regarding mindset. This is what he shared.

Wealth and Mindset by Thaddeus J. Garrett Author of "The Relentless Cultivation of You"

What is a Mindset?

A mindset is a lens through which you view the world. What have you been exposed to? How do you feel about yourself? Who or what are your resources? These things can slightly alter what you see and how you think about your life.

Mindsets are comprised of beliefs, perceptions, and attitudes that inform your thoughts and decisions. Simply speaking, how you move through life.

An open mindset can be an important part of your development for success. It can enhance your path or bring clarity to obstacles on the road ahead.

Cultivating a healthy wealth mindset will help you stick to your financial goals and find ways to increase your earning potential. Let's get to work!

A wealth mindset is a set of beliefs, habits, and behaviors that separates the wealthy from the rest. A wealth mindset will guide you to make the most of the money you have. But let's be clear, wealth does not equate to money only.

Cultivating the Mindset

If you have not researched wealthy people, it's my suggestion that you do. We cannot become what we don't understand or don't have access to.

Here are a few statistics I must share with you. You can do a deeper dive into the statistics of the wealthy.

- The United States added 2,251,000 new millionaires from 2019 to 2020.
- The total number of millionaires in the US is 20.27 million.
- There are 788 billionaires in the United States.
- There are 323,443 millionaire households in New Jersey.
- 76% of US millionaires are white.
- 43.4% of the world's wealth is controlled by the top 1%.
- The Global Wealth Report says that the total number of millionaires in the US is 20.27 million.
- The United States also added 2,251,000 new millionaires from 2019 to 2020 alone, which puts it at the very top of the list of countries with the most millionaires.
- The adult US population is around 250 million, which means that just over 8% of Americans are millionaires.
- Only about 20% of Americans inherit their riches.
- The rest of them (80%) are self-made, first-generation millionaires.

Most millionaires must work for their money and don't get rich once a relative dies, according to "The Millionaire Next Door: The Surprising Secrets of America's Wealthy" by Thomas J Stanley.

86

According to a census report in 2020, there are 788 billionaires in the United States with a combined net worth of $3.431 trillion. In contrast, the United States had 404 billionaires in 2010.

According to the most recent data available, 76% of US millionaires were white or Caucasian. Black American and Asian millionaires each accounted for just 8%. Hispanics made up 7% of the total millionaire population.

Now that you have some actual data ask yourself where you fit into the world of Millionaires and the wealthy. The first step to a wealth mindset is knowing the data behind wealth and implementing the appropriate strategies to achieve your goals.

To be clear you must understand where you are and where you want to go. Very few wealthy people became rich overnight.

Building wealth is a slow process.

Don't get your hopes up on achieving wealth on risky "get rich quick" ventures. Here are some well-known brands that started with one person, one idea, one action, and became household names even today: Ford, Hershey's, Mars, Walmart, Tesla, Disney, and Porsche, just to highlight a few. Food for thought, each of the listed brands is the actual name of a person. Each one of these brands started with the vision, effort, and the quick attitude of one person.

Cultivating the Mindset

The moral of the story is mindset is powerful. Change yours and become the next household name.

Now that you have some tangible information and actual examples of people who demonstrated a wealth mindset, it's time to invest in the most important thing: YOU!

If you want to foster a wealth mindset, you'll need to minimize time-wasting activities like watching television or scrolling through social media. Globally, we spend too much time on devices for pleasure and not research and personal development.

Instead of wasting that time scrolling for the latest social media trend take care of your body. If you are already focusing on your mental and physical health, learn and practice better health habits such as eating healthy, sleeping right, and exercising the right way. I wish mental relief and wellness to you all.

Another great wealth mindset strategy is to practice your negotiation skills. Whether it's negotiating your bills, your salary, or a client contract, wealthy people always come out on top and can squeeze more dollars for themselves based on value.

The best sells are the ones where both the seller and the buyer both obtain what they expect from the deal. Both parties win! The power of negotiation is key to a wealth mindset.

Passion: strong liking or desire.

Find a niche you're passionate about and it won't even feel like work. Learn new skills in areas you're interested in too. You never know when a skill you learned today will become an opportunity later down the line. Remember sometimes you must move in fear.

Some of you have heard of the "law of attraction."

The law of attraction states that like attracts like. In other words, our thoughts and actions attract similar thoughts and actions. If you think it, you can become it. Mind power is everything.

If you think positive thoughts, positive things will happen. If you think about creating wealth, you will bring more wealth into your life. You must foster positive thoughts of wealth and abundance. If you dwell on the negative, you'll get discouraged and give up on your dreams.

Start by erasing negative thoughts from your mind. Some people cannot see themselves as wealthy, some people have a fear of wealth, and some people even suggest wealth is evil.

Replace the negative thoughts, start to understand your true passion, live within those passions, and all aspects of wealth will come to you organically. You will succeed and live your wildest thoughts!

The road to wealth mindset isn't easy, but it won't be any easier if you start creating potholes for yourself. You need to be completely sold on the idea of your successful mindset.

How long does it take to develop a Wealth Mindset?

The best part of developing a wealth mindset is that you can start immediately—by education, strategizing, and then action. Conceptualize, implement, analyze, then redo! It's a formula. You do not change your mindset by chance; you must be direct and intentional. The key is to just start!

Make It Happen

There's no simple formula to follow for wealth. Maybe you'll have a brilliant idea and see it through. Maybe you'll start a business. Maybe you'll work hard, save smart, and invest your way into riches.

At the end of the day, everyone must take the route that's right for them.

However, those who make it to the end will be the individuals who are able to develop, share with others, and stick to the wealth mindset.

Chapter Ten

The Harvest

Most people never wonder what the difference is between having money and having wealth. They go through life with the sole purpose of earning enough money to ensure they have a good living. Yet most people are at or just above the poverty line.

As long as the rent is paid (I am saying rent purposefully), food is on the table, and the minimum on the credit cards are met, they are okay.

There's no doubt about it, earning a good income is great. But "having money" and "wealth creation" are really two different things. Income pays the bills, but it's money that goes into your pocket and right back out. When you have wealth—savings, assets, and investments—you have more than just income.

Wealth is a set of resources you can use to create and take advantage of life's opportunities for generations.

Most people do not think about retirement. Back in the day (Can I say that?), the basics on retirement planning and pension benefits, such as how Social Security works, retiring from the civil service, and managing a private pension, was a small part of our society. Today companies have moved toward 401K and similar plans that only mimic the retirement of old. (Don't count on it alone!)

I AM NOT attacking retirement planning. I AM NOT. Wealth creation will consist of elements needed for those who seek retirement. So, let's look at some foundational principles that you may have learned over the years.

I want to share some actions that could help bolster your portfolio as you approach your planned retirement date if you start now. After all, you have been working and saving for decades, right? Hopefully, you can finally see retirement on the horizon.

Many times, I discover that people begin to coast before it's time to do so. If you plan to retire within the next 10 years or so, it is recommended that you consider taking certain steps now to help ensure you have what you need to enjoy a comfortable retirement lifestyle. (Retirement, not Wealth Creation.)

You must examine your income sources well in advance of your target retirement date. This should give you time to make any necessary adjustments. (The same as with Wealth Creation.) You must envision the kind of retirement you want. Will you work part-time, volunteer, travel? (Not recommended for Wealth Creation.)

Of course, you must develop a realistic picture of the financial resources you may need and then determine if your current resources will be sufficient to support your plan. If you find there is a gap, think about how to accumulate the additional assets you need or adjust your vision to match your resources.

By analyzing your current expenses, you may identify discretionary items that can be eliminated or reduced. If you look at everything you purchase over the course of a month, you may be surprised by how much you can cut back to have more money to invest for your retirement.

When your goal is to retire, it can be tempting to shy away from stocks to reduce risk. But the growth that stocks can provide is still important at this stage of your life. Consider maintaining a sound mix of stocks, bonds, crypto, bitcoin, mutual funds, and other assets that fit your risk tolerance, investment time horizon, and liquidity needs.

A well-balanced portfolio may help you weather downturns and potentially generate the kind of income that you will need to cover expenses in a retirement that could last more than three decades. (This is a great assessment for both retirement and wealth creation.)

Let me be clear here. Just because you consider your efforts to diversify your portfolio, please note that diversification does not ensure a profit or protect against loss in declining markets.

You may have noticed the market has had a number of declining days in 2022, in addition to inflation, price increases, and a war.

The Harvest

Wealth creation usually doesn't happen overnight, in a year, or in three years. Creating wealth is a series of steps that you take over time. It's an ongoing process that requires discipline.

If you apply these disciplines, wealth creation becomes a life pattern. As you move through each stage of life, you will grow in your ability to create wealth and to pass that wealth **from generation to generation**. (Please read that again.)

The steps to wealth creation involve following a life pattern, a discipline, and a process. Most people quit and become discouraged just hearing about these steps. After all, this is not new information. What will make this new, or should I say doable, is the fact that you are ready for a harvest in your financial life.

Earlier, I asked the question: Did you know that a seed is dead/dormant until it is placed in the right environment? One of my best friends is renowned speaker, Les Brown. For years, he has challenged and directed people to look deep inside of themselves. One of his many powerful quotes is, "You have greatness in YOU."

There are seeds inside of you that are dead and lying dormant. They are not sitting in the right environment therefore, do not expect to receive anything. You have seed inside of you. This is that stage in life that you must discover that one thing deep inside of you.

After recognizing your seed and purpose, focus on creating and managing the various levels of cash flow. Before anyone can truly begin building and creating wealth, they must consistently generate enough income to handle not only month-to-month expenses, but day-to-day. It's also a good idea to have enough **savings** set aside to cover at least 6 months and if possible, nine months to a year of living expenses, in case of a financial emergency.

I am not going to take you back to my book "Wealth Increasing Now," even though I should. Strong cash flow management comes from establishing a sound budget. If you are reading this and do not have a budget, put the book down, walk away from it, and do not attempt to move forward. Seriously, one of the primary reasons that most people are not successful is that they are looking for shortcuts. There are none in wealth creation; it is a deliberate process.

So many are stuck and can't envision the difference between living for now and wealth creation. Without having the most powerful tool, a budget, you cannot experience that positive cash flow.

You have heard a thousand times that the amount of money coming in must exceed the amount going out. Understanding your **life pattern** and your **cash flow pattern** is critical to wealth creation. Do you see the pattern that I am trying to create for you?

Unfortunately, there is a pattern that most people relate to: money flowing in as your salary income only and flowing out to pay expenses and debt. None of this income is saved or invested.

It's just allowing you to meet your obligations and maybe, just maybe, save a little here and there.

Whenever there is a lack of or little savings, it can cause obvious problems. The main problem is that there's no capital being stored away for a rainy day, no wealth being accumulated, and no money set aside to prepare for retirement or anything else.

Yes, this cash flow pattern may support living an enjoyable lifestyle. It won't, however, lead to an increase in wealth at the end of each year, which may lead to a lower standard of living during retirement.

Now, let's look at another process of cash flow. In this process, money flows in as salary and flows out to pay expenses and invest. I call this "cash-creating assets." The key is that the flow of money from these assets is an additional source of income.

When you begin to invest in assets such as term deposits, shares, investment properties, managed funds, crypto, and bitcoin, it is possible to create cash to add to your other income.

There may be further benefits available from these investments as well, such as reduction in the amount of tax you pay—which means more of your money is working to achieve your goals.

At this point, you can see and relate to two cash flow patterns. While many people focus only on the short-term, to achieve genuine financial success, and all the lifestyle benefits that go with it, you need to manage your cash so that it grows and creates income.

This could involve creating positive cash flow by investing in cash-creating assets. These assets are commonly managed through a cash management account which acts as a central hub. I'll share more about this later.

By doing this, you can potentially create an additional source of income over and above the salary you earn. That is what wealth creation is all about. Please be mindful that none of this is about how much you earn in salary. It is about what you consistently do with your income.

Remember, none of this will take place if the foundation is not established. Having the cash flow foundation in place, you can begin to direct your efforts towards creating your long-term vision and clear goals for the future you want.

You are able to invest in assets. Investments such as real estate, stocks, crypto, bitcoin, and insurance investments, increase in value time over time and allow you to enjoy a comfortable lifestyle and generational wealth at some point in the future.

Can you now see what you should be trying to achieve and how all the major pieces of your financial world add up into one complete picture?

The Harvest

This is the real reason to earn an income. It is not about bills, debts, and obligations. It is about wealth creation.

I often have conversations with one of my cousins who is like a brother to me. He is a truck driver, but not just any truck driver; his work is a specialty. He uniquely transports multiple trucks and his van at the same time.

This not about his work, it's about his earnings. There are so many contractors, business owners, and commission earners who can actually control how much their earnings can be in a given week or month.

Here is my question to him and each of you. "WHY" are you not creating enough income to escalate your ability to invest? You really should ponder this and consider making the necessary changes to begin wealth creation.

I can say this a thousand times and it still will not reach the masses: It is not about the money. If it was, this would never be a conversation. Heck, you're already earning good money and are asset poor. It's about the mindset.

I am going to start talking digital assets as we move forward and some of you are already turned off about the idea. Mindset!

Chapter Eleven

Wealth Creation

Finally, what you have been waiting for: the steps that will help you establish wealth creation that will change your life. From the very beginning I started by telling you this thing (Mindset) is mental.

Your mindset, values, and attitudes around money affect all elements of your life. The core principle of who you are, the character ethic that is deep inside of you, must now take action.

I am not going to talk about a budget. I will use some language I do not necessarily like to use about money, like disposable income, and how to best use your money, in addition to educating yourself and remembering that your previous money skills were learned behavior. It is this new learned behavior along with your value systems that will allow you to be successful.

Wealth is commonly identified as a state of having an abundant supply of material goods, especially money. Wealth creating is bigger than a financial goal, a short-term savings plan, or a deposit on the purchase of your first home.

Those are excellent things to accomplish and they should serve as foundational things that you have in place. But wealth creation includes more complex goals like early repayment of a mortgage or putting a strategy in place to achieve financial freedom. Wealth creation is about generational wealth and wealth transfer.

As stated before, the purpose of this series is to help make money work for you, rather than the other way around. To do this, you need to understand the benefits of compound interest and saving money to invest, while still ensuring you can enjoy the quality of life that you want.

To maximize the benefits of compound interest, it is better to start early. It's not optional; it's a relevant wealth creation strategy that will work for you.

Before you begin investing, you need to know the reason behind it. Your purpose will direct you to your goals even before you start acting on the best practices of investing.

Wealth creation is commonly done for financial security. It matters that your concept of financial security is clear when investing, so when markets get volatile like you have witnessed in 2022, you can always remind yourself of your reason behind investing, and you can gauge if you have achieved financial security.

Clarify your "*WHY*"

I am not going to try to give you your reasons why you should pursue wealth creation for yourself. This is truly your moment to establish your legacy and reasons WHY you want to be uniquely different from those who have held you back.

In the very beginning I asked, "WHY?" Now it is time for your answer.

It may seem easy to find the answers to the many questions that can form from "What is your why?" You may even think that the mission/vision/values statements that others are telling you that you should write are enough. But no, it's not. Your why—your core belief, your purpose—is the answer. Everything else comes afterward—and becomes so much easier to define.

Never try to dress it up. When you do, you will find yourself feeling empty and uninspired after every unfulfilled moment. I recommend you sit down and rethink, "WHY am I seeking what I am seeking?" Don't expect it to be perfect. When you have your purpose in mind, you really feel very proud of what you want to do.

Do not just settle with being a wealth creator, be a foundation builder with a mission. You should want to ensure that your decision will impact the lives of others. You should want to educate them on your process and success in order to inspire them. Say no to anything that pulls you away from this purpose and take advantage of every opportunity that supports this purpose.

Your why is your purpose. It is your reason for getting up in the morning. It is what motivates you to action. It is what keeps you focused each and every day. That old mindset has you getting up every morning, getting dressed, hurrying to get to a job that you do not like, and being around people who have little to no values or purposes. However, each of you were still likeminded because you just wanted to earn enough to pay the bills.

No one has the power to take your purpose from you. But while it is yours, many can share your purpose. Aligning shared passions, shared beliefs, and shared values is how one finds common purpose.

Purposeful leaders leverage common purpose to inspire, unify, and drive collective action to achieve their goals and desired outcomes. This is who you are, you are the leader of your environment. Purpose-driven brands find the common purpose across organizational stakeholders, their customers, and society, to achieve business sustainability and make a positive impact in the world.

Every individual should have a purpose. While you are beginning to identify your purpose, it does not mean it does not exist. If you are constantly stressed, demotivated, unfulfilled at work, pessimistic of the world, or feel your life lacks meaning, these are clear indicators that you are not living your purpose.

If your company does not appreciate its employees, possesses a negative culture, focuses solely on increasing margins, and operates in silos, it means your company has not yet aligned around a common purpose. The good news is that it is never too late to find your purpose.

I found my purpose less than fifteen years ago. Once I did, I can honestly say I have never been happier and life has never been more fulfilling—both personally and professionally.

Understand yourself

What do you know about yourself, really? I want you to survey your surroundings and relationships in relation to the purposes you claim are your WHY. Be honest with yourself. Do they line up? Are you really turning things around? Have things really changed with you?

Understand your learning style. There is a theory that every person learns and processes their experiences in different ways. Knowing your learning style will help you understand why you struggle with some activities and excel at others.

It is so important that as you settle on your WHY that you evaluate your strengths and weaknesses. You can come to a better understanding of who you are and what is most important to you by thinking about your strengths and weaknesses.

Equally importantly, you'll want to compare your perception of your strengths and weaknesses to the strengths and weaknesses identified by your friends, family, and coworkers.

The things they see that you don't can tell you a lot about yourself and how you see yourself. I am not speaking of your family, friends, and coworkers giving you their thoughts about wealth creation. No, no, no.

I believe that oftentimes, you are so busy with building and creating a frame around you that you never get a chance to see the picture—your big picture, your real self. Your big picture includes your strengths, determination, devotion, self-discipline, thoughtfulness, decisiveness, patience, diplomacy, communication skills, and imagination or creativity.

Because so many never consider their strengths, they are heavily focused on their weaknesses, which could include close-mindedness, self-centeredness, difficulty perceiving reality, judgment of others, and issues with control. Wealth creation is rarely built in this type of environment.

Selecting Investment Products

By now you should have a great idea of what type of strategy you want to employ around your investment goals. If you have not, please move in that direction before moving forward. Remember this book is about your mindset in this wealth creation space and you must feel good about it.

Write down the financial goals that you want to establish and create a strategy for each one that allows you to level up.

Here is an example of what I mean by establishing a strategy that will allow you to level up on whatever your financial goals are. Many years ago, I opened up a bank account and started a certificate of deposit (CD) at that bank. I realized that each month I would make an $88 payment towards a $1,000 CD over the course of one year. And each year, I had a 10-day grace period for which I would be able to cash in or reassign that CD.

The goal was to use what most of us call the latter approach. With this approach, you open a CD and when you begin to reach your goals, you build, go to the next step, and continue that process. At this stage of your wealth creation what you want to do is the same thing. Begin the process regardless of how small or large. Create a process with a goal and each time you will level up and go higher.

When we talk about stocks and stock ownership we're referring to products that will provide dividend payments. These dividend payments will be reinvested, resulting in a compounding effect. As you select stocks and create your strategy towards managing and reaching your financial goals of wealth creation, each opportunity should give you the ability to level up.

Devising a strategy for choosing investments appropriate for each of your investment goals, is taking a major step towards meeting them. Please, do not take this moment lightly. This can really be your moment to change the cycle of generational wealth in your favor.

Whether you decide to use an investment professional or not, it's important to understand what your investment choices are and how different types of investments put your money to work. It's equally important to understand yourself as an investor—I just talked about this. This is important because a portfolio that's right for someone else may not be best for you.

Some factors that can make a difference in your investment selection are your goals, or what you want to accomplish by investing, and the time frames for meeting those goals. It's also important to have a handle on your risk tolerance, which is your attitude towards risk.

Let me be clear, there is no single approach to choosing investments that will work for everyone or be right for every situation. However, here are a few tried-and-true rules for sound investment selection.

Know what you own. Focus on investments that are easy for you to evaluate and give you access to reliable information about them. Regulators require that certain information be disclosed to investors through documents such as offering circulars, mutual fund prospectuses, and corporate filings for stock issued by public companies that trade on the major stock markets. In addition, you can find a wealth of real-time and historical market data for stocks, bonds, mutual funds, and other securities online.

Assess liquidity. Make sure there is a market to trade your investments. Highly liquid investments are easy to buy and sell, either through a brokerage account or directly from the issuer in some cases. Thinly traded stocks or securities that aren't listed on a national securities exchange tend to be less liquid and are rarely a good idea for most investors, seasoned or not.

Likewise, exercise caution when considering securities such as non-traded REITs that may be illiquid—meaning you can't get cash out of them even if you really need to—for long periods of time.

Know the true cost. Have a clear understanding of any costs, sales charges, and fees involved with buying and selling investment products, including whether there are penalties or additional fees for selling your investment within a certain time frame.

Understanding risk is key. When you select any investment product, it's vital to understand that all investments carry some level of risk. Stocks, bonds, mutual funds, and exchange-traded funds (ETFs) can lose value—even all of their value—if market conditions sour.

Even conservative, insured investments, such as certificates of deposit (CDs) issued by a bank or credit union, come with inflation risk. They may not earn enough over time to keep pace with the increasing cost of living. Whatever investment you're considering, be sure you know how it can make or lose money before you buy.

Risk is uncertainty with respect to your investments that has the potential to negatively affect your financial welfare. For example, your investment value might rise or fall because of market conditions (market risk). The first and second quarters of 2022 are proof.

Corporate decisions, such as whether to expand into a new area of business or merge with another company, can also affect the value of your investments (business risk). If you own an international investment, events within that country can affect your investment (political risk and currency risk).

There are other types of risk to consider. How easy or hard it is to cash out of an investment when you need to is called liquidity risk. Another risk factor is tied to how many or how few investments you hold. Generally speaking, the more financial eggs you have in one basket (say, all your money in a single stock), the greater risk you take (concentration risk).

Time frames and investment selection

For every financial goal you set, think about the time frame in which you might need the money you have invested. For near-term goals, you'll want to consider moving some or all of your portfolio into liquid, lower-volatility investments such as short-term bonds, certificates of deposit, and cash.

For longer-term goals, stocks and mutual funds that invest in stocks have the potential to provide higher returns. Based on historical data, holding a broad portfolio of stocks over an extended period of time (for instance, a large-cap portfolio like the S&P 500 over a 20-year period) significantly reduces your chances of losing your principal. However, the historical data should not mislead investors into thinking that there is no risk in investing in stocks over a long period of time.

As an investor, you should consider how realistic it will be for you to ride out the ups and downs of the market over the long term. Will you have to sell stocks during an economic downturn to fill the gap caused by a job loss? Will you sell investments to pay for medical care or a child's college education?

Predictable and unpredictable life events might make it difficult for you to stay invested in stocks over an extended period of time. This is why I am asking you to consider every aspect.

Here's the bottom line: At every stage of your investing life, the more carefully you plan and the more informed the investment decisions you make, the better the chances you'll have of meeting all of your investment goals and achieving a secure financial future.

Investing in the stock market has historically been one of the most important pathways to financial success. As you dive into researching stocks, you'll often hear them discussed with reference to different categories of stocks and different classifications. Here are the major types of stocks you should know.

Common stock	Dividend stocks
Preferred stock	Non-dividend stocks
Large-cap stocks	Income stocks
Mid-cap stocks	Cyclical stocks
Small-cap stocks	Non-cyclical stocks
Domestic stocks	Safe stocks
International stocks	ESG stocks
Growth stocks	Blue chip stocks
Value stocks	Penny stocks
IPO stocks	

Most stock that people invest in is common stock. **Common stock** represents partial ownership in a company, with shareholders getting the right to receive a proportional share of the value of any remaining assets if the company gets dissolved. Common stock gives shareholders theoretically unlimited upside potential, but they also risk losing everything if the company fails without having any assets left over.

Preferred stock works differently, as it gives shareholders a preference over common shareholders to get back a certain amount of money if the company dissolves. Preferred shareholders also have the right to receive dividend payments before common shareholders do.

The net result is that preferred stock as an investment often more closely resembles fixed-income bond investments than regular common stock. Often, a company will offer only common stock. This makes sense, as that is what shareholders most often seek to buy.

Large-cap, Mid-cap, and Small-cap stocks

Stocks also get categorized by the total worth of all their shares, which is called market capitalization. Companies with the biggest market capitalizations are called large-cap stocks, with mid-cap and small-cap stocks representing successively smaller companies.

There's no precise line that separates these categories from each other. However, one often-used rule is that stocks with market capitalizations of $10 billion or more are treated as large-caps, with stocks having market caps between $2 billion and $10 billion qualifying as mid-caps and stocks with market caps below $2 billion getting treated as small-cap stocks.

Large-cap stocks are generally considered safer and more conservative as investments, while mid-caps and small-caps have greater capacity for future growth but are riskier. However, just because two companies fall into the same category, it doesn't mean they have anything else in common as investments or that they'll perform in similar ways in the future.

Make your portfolio reflect your best vision for the future.

Domestic stocks and International stocks

You can categorize stocks by where they're located. For purposes of distinguishing domestic U.S. stocks from international stocks, most investors look at the location of the company's official headquarters.

However, it's important to understand that a stock's geographical category doesn't necessarily correspond to where the company gets its sales. Philip Morris International (NYSE:PM) is a great example, as its headquarters are in the U.S., but it sells its tobacco and other products exclusively outside the country.

It can be hard to tell from business operations and financial metrics whether a company is truly domestic or international, especially among large multinational corporations.

Growth stocks and Value stocks

Another categorization method distinguishes two popular investment methods. Growth investors tend to look for companies that are seeing their sales and profits rise quickly.

Value investors look for companies whose shares are inexpensive, whether relative to their peers or to their own past stock price.

Growth stocks tend to have higher risk levels, but the potential returns can be extremely attractive. Successful growth stocks have businesses that tap into strong and rising demand among customers, especially in connection with longer-term trends throughout society that support the use of their products and services.

Competition can be fierce, though, and if rivals disrupt a growth stock's business, it can fall from favor quickly. Sometimes, even just a growth slowdown is enough to send prices sharply lower, as investors fear that long-term growth potential is waning.

Value stocks, on the other hand, are seen as being more conservative investments. They're often mature, well-known companies that have already grown into industry leaders and therefore don't have as much room left to expand further. Yet with reliable business models that have stood the test of time, they can be good choices for those seeking more price stability while still getting some of the positives of exposure to stocks.

IPO stocks

IPO stocks are stocks of companies that have recently gone public through an initial public offering. IPOs often generate a lot of excitement among investors looking to get in on the ground floor of a promising business concept. But they can also be volatile, especially when there's disagreement within the investment community about their prospects for growth and profit. A stock generally retains its status as an IPO stock for at least a year and for as long as two to four years after it becomes public.

Dividend stocks and Non-dividend stocks

Many stocks make dividend payments to their shareholders on a regular basis. Dividends provide valuable income for investors, and that makes dividend stocks highly sought after among certain investment circles. Technically, paying even $0.01 per share qualifies a company as a dividend stock.

However, stocks don't have to pay dividends. Non-dividend stocks can still be strong investments if their prices rise over time. Some of the biggest companies in the world don't pay dividends, although the trend in recent years has been towards more stocks making dividend payouts to their shareholders.

Income stocks

Income stocks are another name for dividend stocks, as the income that most stocks pay out comes in the form of dividends. However, income stocks also refer to shares of companies that have more mature business models and have relatively fewer long-term opportunities for growth. Ideal for conservative investors who need to draw cash from their investment portfolios right now, income stocks are a favorite among those in or nearing retirement.

Cyclical stocks and Non-cyclical stocks

National economies tend to follow cycles of expansion and contraction, with periods of prosperity and recession. Certain businesses have greater exposure to broad business cycles, and investors therefore refer to them as cyclical stocks.

Cyclical stocks include shares of companies in industries like manufacturing, travel, and luxury goods, because an economic downturn can take away customers' ability to make major purchases quickly. When economies are strong, however, a rush of demand can make these companies rebound sharply.

By contrast, non-cyclical stocks, also known as secular or defensive stocks, don't have those big swings in demand. An example would be grocery store chains, because no matter how good or bad the economy is, people still have to eat. Non-cyclical stocks tend to perform better during market downturns, while cyclical stocks often outperform during strong bull markets.

Safe stocks

Safe stocks are stocks whose share prices make relatively small movements up and down compared to the overall stock market. Also known as low-volatility stocks, safe stocks typically operate in industries that aren't as sensitive to changing economic conditions. They often pay dividends as well, and that income can offset falling share prices during tough times.

Stock market sectors

You'll often see stocks broken down by the type of business they're in. The basic categories most often used include stock market sectors. This is an excellent way for you to target various sectors and build unique portfolios. Understanding different categories of stocks is key to building a strong portfolio.

- Communication Services—telephone, internet, media, and entertainment companies
- Consumer Discretionary—retailers, automakers, and hotel and restaurant companies
- Consumer Staples—food, beverage, tobacco, and household and personal products companies
- Energy—oil, and gas exploration and production companies, pipeline providers, and gas station operators
- Financial—banks, mortgage finance specialists, and insurance and brokerage companies
- Healthcare—health insurers, drug and biotech companies, and medical device makers
- Industrial—airlines, aerospace and defense, construction, logistics, machinery, and railroad companies
- Materials—mining, forest products, construction materials, packaging, and chemical companies
- Real Estate—real estate investment trusts and real estate management and development companies

- Technology—hardware, software, semiconductor, communications equipment, and IT services companies
- Utilities—electric, natural gas, water, renewable energy, and multi-product utility companies
- Stock Exchanges—Exchanges are where you buy and sell shares of stock.
- Stock Market Indexes—Indexes illustrate stock prices for a variety of companies across industries.

ESG Investing

ESG Investing refers to an investment philosophy that puts emphasis on environmental, social, and governance concerns. Rather than focusing entirely on whether a company generates profit and is growing its revenue over time, ESG principles consider other collateral impacts on the environment, company employees, customers, and shareholder rights.

Tied to ESG's governing rules is socially responsible investing, or SRI. Investors using SRI screen out stocks of companies that don't match up to their most important values.

However, ESG investing has a more positive element in that rather than simply excluding companies that fail key tests, it actively encourages investing in the companies that do things the best. With evidence showing that a clear commitment to ESG principles can improve investing returns, there's a lot of interest in the area.

Blue Chip stocks and Penny stocks

Finally, there are stock categories that make judgments based on perceived quality. Blue chip stocks tend to be the cream of the crop in the business world, featuring companies that lead their respective industries and have gained strong reputations.

They typically don't provide the absolute highest returns, but their stability makes them favorites among investors with lower tolerance for risk.

By contrast, penny stocks are low-quality companies whose stock prices are extremely inexpensive, typically less than $1 per share. With dangerously speculative business models, penny stocks are prone to schemes that can drain your entire investment. It's important to know about the dangers of penny stocks.

Here is a habit exercise that will allow you to create wealth with a direct focus. It has nothing to do with talent, skills, or luck for that matter. It's all about being intentional.

Each week follow the guide below and purchase at least the number of shares of the type of stocks for the week listed. You will be creating your personal portfolio of stocks.

These stocks are for long term purposes. Following this exercise and creating a habit will carry value for you in your financial future. You do not have to do this, though.

Your stock purchase schedule: No minimum or maximum price.

Common stock   Buy Minimum 1 Share Week 1 & 22, 43
Preferred stock   Buy Minimum 2 Share Week 2 & 23, 44
Large-cap stocks   Buy Minimum 3 Share Week 3 & 24, 45
Mid-cap stocks   Buy Minimum 4 Share Week 4 & 25, 46
Small-cap stocks   Buy Minimum 5 Share Week 5 & 26, 47
Domestic stocks   Buy Minimum 1 Share Week 6 & 27, 48
International stocks Buy Minimum 2 Share Week 7 & 28
Growth stocks   Buy Minimum 3 Share Week 8 & 29, 49
Value stocks   Buy Minimum 4 Share Week 9 & 30
IPO stocks   Buy Minimum 5 Share Week 10 & 31
Dividend stocks   Buy Minimum 1 Share Week 11 & 32, 50
Non-dividend stocks Buy Minimum 2 Share Week 12 & 33
Income stocks   Buy Minimum 3 Share Week 13 & 34, 51
Cyclical stocks   Buy Minimum 4 Share Week 14 & 35

Non-cyclical stocks Buy Minimum 5 Share Week 15 & 36
Safe stocks   Buy Minimum 1 Share Week 16 & 37
ESG stocks   Buy Minimum 2 Share Week 17 & 38
Blue chip stocks   Buy Minimum 3 Share Week 18 & 39
Penny stocks   Buy Minimum 4 Share Week 19 & 40, 52
Common stock   Buy Minimum 5 Share Week 20 & 41
Preferred stock   Buy Minimum 1 Share Week 21 & 42

If by chance you decide to complete this exercise, you should end up with a portfolio of 21 types of stocks and a total of over 85 shares of stocks.

Chapter Twelve

Bonus

I know this is about mindset, but I want you to realize there is a path for you to follow. The more information that you have, the better you will be able to create wealth.

Remember, a strong mindset is what allows you to stay focused on your intentions, instead of negative thoughts. It's what helps you understand that struggle is impermanent and won't derail your success. It keeps you from making self-destructive decisions. Investing in the stock market requires you to be strong.

If you have not already started, create habits daily to help your mind retain a pattern. It really takes 21 days to establish a pattern. But the longer and more consistently you work to keep this habit, the better your mind will be at scanning the world for the positive.

The stock market and investing will be a way of life. The mind is just like a muscle—the more you exercise it, the stronger it gets and the more it can expand. The mind has a powerful way of attracting things that are in harmony with it, good and bad. Mindset…

The Bonus

I'm always more successful when I focus on creating new habits. Turn this into a game and find a time each day to learn. It could be at mealtime, in the car on the way to work or practice, maybe even as part of your bedtime routine. Remember a positive mindset is more creative, more productive, and more engaged. Isn't that exactly what you want?

Stocks are one of the most interesting, lucrative, and equally risky forms of investment. People decide to buy stocks with the hope of gaining good returns. Many, like Warren Buffet, have even made billions by trading, while many have also had bitter experiences while investing in stocks. Therefore, careful understanding of stocks is mandatory before going into the market, as there are many different types of stocks which have their own benefits and disadvantages as well.

Income Stocks

An income stock is an equity security that offers high yield that may generate the majority of the security's overall returns. It is a very popular type of stock among investors since it is least volatile among all and offers higher-than-market dividend yield to its investors.

Income stocks are usually issued by large and well-established organizations that possess an impressive track record of managing their business operations and finances. Moreover, whenever a large organization makes some profit, most of its portion goes to the investors instead of being reinvested into the company. This is why many of the income stocks are considered as "Blue Chip" stocks. They provide a consistent, fairly reliable, and handsome dividend to investors.

Income stocks can be found in any industry but it is usually available in traditionally stable sectors like real estate, energy sector, utilities, financial institutions, natural resources, and food among others.

People who do not have a regular source of income and want to earn money with low risk are often attracted to this type of stock. Older or retired people are among those who invest heavily in income stocks. An ideal income stock has very low volatility, dividends higher than the prevailing 10-year treasury bond rates, and a modest level of annual profit growth.

Penny Stocks

Penny stocks are usually issued by small companies, especially start-ups, to raise funds from the investors. This type of stock is usually illiquid, are traded at a very low price, and issued by companies that have very low market capitalization.

In the Indian trading market, penny stocks are usually traded below the price of one rupee. In western markets, such stocks usually trade below $1. Many also consider a stock priced under $5 as a penny stock.

The benefit of investing in penny stocks is that it is available at a low price and has the potential to turn a small investment into a fortune. For example, if you purchase 50,000 shares of a penny stock at a price of $1 each, even a $1 rise in the share price can lead you to earn $50,000 in a limited time.

However, as people say, every good thing comes with some risk. Here's something to keep in mind. Penny stocks are considered risky as they come from companies with fewer shareholders and disclose very limited information about their businesses. Moreover, such types of stocks are more prone to price manipulation and scams and usually do not end up making money for investors.

Speculative Stocks

Speculative stocks are stocks issued by companies that are developing new products, want to tap unexplored territory (often foreign markets), or have made major changes to their management or financial level.

Such stocks usually carry high risk as the company, product, and management is often untested. Many do not succeed in the long run but if such companies do succeed, the return on investment could be very high. It gives a promise of high return but the risk is also high.

Growth Stocks

With growth stocks, any profit that a company earns gets reinvested into the company itself to boost its innovation and business expansion. Investors do not get any dividends with this type of stock. Instead, they receive capital gain whenever they sell their stock. As the company grows the prices of shares also increases and the investor receives higher capital gain. But when the reverse happens, investors suffer loss as well.

With this type of stocks, loyal customers who trust the company, its product, and management, invest their money for the longer run. Both small and large companies issue growth stocks.

Cyclical Stocks

Stock in companies that offer luxury and discretionary goods and services are often considered as cyclical stocks.

This category includes airlines, vehicle manufactures, hotels, restaurants, and clothing among others. Performances of such stocks are interlinked with the health of the economy.

When the economy does well, prices of such stocks usually remain high. When it performs badly, values of stocks lose a substantial value. For example, when the economy flourishes, people can afford to invest in buying cars, buying homes, shopping, and traveling. This causes prices to go up.

When an economic downturn starts, these discretionary expenses are the first ones consumers cut. However, in many cases, prices of Cyclical Stocks increase when the economy recovers after recession and many times surpasses its older value. Many cyclical stocks possess the bounce back capability and are therefore favored among many investors.

Value Stocks

When companies have assets worth more than its stock price, that stock is considered as value stock. Such stocks are seen as undervalued stocks by the investors who believe that the value of its shares will increase over time as the company starts growing. If the company does not do well, losses can also happen.

Defensive Stocks

Food, fuel, and healthcare services are things every human will always need. Even if a recession starts, no one stops eating food, stops refilling their fuel tanks, or avoids going to hospitals. The stocks of such vital services are considered defensive stocks. Such stocks are almost immune to any economic downturn, profit loss, or financial slumps. Its demand increases when the economy gets worse.

In today's times of globalization and fierce competition among rivals, even a small unpleasant event can have a bad effect on the economy. As such, it is the responsibility of the individual investor to understand the nitty-gritty of all types of stocks and other forms of investments before drawing any conclusions. As an investor, smartness and wisdom is what matters at the end of the day. Wealth Creation Mindset.

Chapter Thirteen

My Final Words

As I conclude this book, I want to remind you that I began by talking about how the mindset is mental and how important it is that we understand that many of the things that affect our mindsets come from learned behavior.

The things that have impacted us all of our lives often comes from issues in our lives that we live out daily in our financial life. We are constantly creating hardship that causes us to struggle to pay bills monthly.

We never get the opportunity to become financially independent. We don't know what it is like because we carry too much debt in our lives. Every time we are in a situation where we pay off one bill, we have another bill coming.

We are constantly in a cycle of debt replacing debt. We sometimes feel hopeless. We feel like we are victims who have been victimized by a system that will not allow us to participate in it.

But this is not the case. It all boils down to our mindset and it comes back again to the mental: what we're thinking, how we are thinking, and what has caused us to think in a way that hinders our ability to even consider wealth creation.

The Closing

You have to understand this. There is a breaking point that we have to come to. This breaking point will put us in a position where we actually accept as facts the things that support the mindset that we are hopeless, that we are a victim, and that the system is crushing us. We have to change our mindset.

Our mindset has to move beyond what we are currently operating in. We have to begin to think about wisdom and how we will take this wisdom and expand, build, and create something new for our lives.

All of this must be purposeful. We can't do it without having a devoted commitment to succeed in the things that we want to accomplish financially.

We must have the confidence in purpose, knowing that we can now begin to invest, we can now save money, we can now own multiple properties, we can now create an inheritance for the next generation, and we can now create wealth (not build wealth) and let wealth build upon the wealth that we create.

It's all about the mindset and the formality of the mindset. We have to recognize that the Personality Ethic I talked about earlier in the book, claims "This is who I am," and "This is what I've always done." That thinking is that of a fixed mindset. We really must understand that this fixed mindset has to be broken.

We begin to look at the Character Ethic of what it is that we want to do and ask: Are we doing this based on values or is our decision based on ethics? WHY are we doing it and what are we doing it for? What is our WHY?

Now you've just planted the seed and this seed has to be cultivated. I talked about cultivating the mind. There's so much that you have to do in cultivating your own personal mindset.

This is important for you as you go about building a foundation of understanding that now is the time for you to have a wealth consciousness. It is time to move from poverty to wealth consciousness.

Now your mindset has to be cultivated. You have to learn new things, you have to create new habits, you have to begin to expect a harvest, and you have to begin to understand that when you plant a seed using your money, your money will begin creating money for you.

You are now putting yourself in a position to understand that every action is about you cultivating your mindset. You begin to understand that receiving the harvest prepares you to move into the next phase of true wealth creation. You have to understand what your value system is in order to be able to begin to create wealth. Please hear me: You have to know your values in order to commit to wealth creation.

It's not going to happen by chance. Wealth creation is going to be a systematic process. It's going to be the mechanics of everything that you do—how you wake up in the morning, what you focus on, your actions, your thoughts, your words, your deeds, how you interact with other people, how you build a circle around you, and how you encounter people and begin to develop core relationships that will allow you to expand in the area in which you want to operate.

The Closing

As the operator, understand that you will not do this by yourself. You will need help in this process of wealth creation. Regardless of the rough things that you've had to overcome in your previous mindset, accept the new things that you are now doing differently.

One of my mentors once said to me, "A bee never tries to convince a fly that honey is better than s***." Please allow this to soak in for a moment. Let me repeat it, "A bee never tries to convince a fly that honey is better than s***."

I can't convince you that wealth creation is better than poverty. I just can't convince you. You have to have a mindset of receiving, believe in that, and then take actions towards it.

Your ability to create wealth begins with your thoughts. Your thoughts lead to your feelings. Your feelings lead to your actions. Your due diligence begins with your focus. This is something that you must want and desire to do.

I am so grateful that you're taking the opportunity to read the 1st book in the series, "Wealth Creation – The Mindset."

I highly recommend you read the next book in the series, "Wealth Creation – The Influencer." This next book will lay down another path to enable you to become financially successful, leaving an inheritance to the next generation and creating wealth in a way that no one in your family has ever done before.

Be sure to follow me on all social media.

WWW.IAMROBWILSON.COM

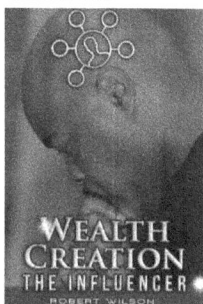

MAKE SURE THAT YOU ARE READING EACH BOOK OF THE SERIES

www.ingramcontent.com/pod-product-compliance
Lightning Source LLC
Chambersburg PA
CBHW060053100426

42742CB00014B/2810